DREAM ON!

JENS BRAMBUSCH

COPYRIGHT

Title: „Dream on!"
Author: Jens Brambusch
Translation: Aannsha & Barry Jones
Cover & Design: Merten Kaatz
Photos: Jim Furness/Jens Brambusch/Özgün Erdem/
SV Delos/Merten Kaatz
Independently published via kdp
ISBN: 9781079726893

Original: „Träum weiter!" (German)
All rights: Jens Brambusch, Moorkamp 45, 29223 Celle

Photo credits: Jim Furness (p. 24, 62, 99, 100, 108, 114, 132), Jens
Brambusch (8, 14, 56, 84, 120, 140, 147, 166), Özgün Erdem (48, 51),
SV Delos (152, 160), private (38, 39, 74, 83), Merten Kaatz (U4, 22)

For the person, who helped me
to make my dream possible.
Even without knowing.

p.s. The writing pad is used up.
I need a new one

ABOUT THE AUTHOR

Jens Brambusch, born in 1972, worked as a reporter at the „Financial Times Deutschland" and later on at the business magazine „Capital". His focus: white collar crime. Some of his reports won prestigious journalism awards. In mid-2018 Brambusch decided to quit his job. He sold his apartment in Berlin, left Germany and bought a sailboat at the Mediterranean - since then he is sailing in Turkey. His personal story you will find in this book: Bye Bye Burnout!

SUMMARY

KAŞ

WINTER

2018/2019

We were strangers.

Stranded in a distant place. Sailors from all over the world, travellers from five continents. Australians, British, Americans, South Africans, Germans and of course Turks. As different as we are in our views, no matter how rich our lives are, whether prosperous or about to go bankrupt, planned or haphazard, private or digital nomad, we all have one thing in common: living our dream.

We live on a sailing ship.

We have left our old life behind us, thrown the ballast of the past overboard - and then set our future course, forever. Or at least for the next few years. None of us know where the wind will take us, where we will be in one, five or even ten years. Some of us want to sail around the world, the others have already circumnavigated half the globe. For some, the Mediterranean means their whole world. Others find their world in just one place.

When we meet for the first time, we are sitting in Oxygen-Pub in the Marina of Kaş, a small town that lies along the historical Lycian Way, a region rich in culture, beautiful anchorages and lovely people. Kaş, somewhere halfway between Marmaris and Antalya, is one of the southernmost points of Turkey. This makes the place attractive for sailors to spend the winter.

When storms rage outside the safety of the harbour or marina, when the blue water of the Mediterranean mounts up to gray walls, Kaş provides security. In the summer in this area, the Mediterranean is as calm as a bath, but in the winter it is an unpredictable beast. Nobody wants to be out there. It was particularly bad in the winter of 2018/2019, of which the Turks say it was the rainiest, coldest and stormiest one they can remember. For the first time, several hurricanes hit the south coast, causing rock falls across major roads, damaging houses and farms and toppling vessels from their winter hard stands causing them to hit the concrete so hard they split open as easily as ripe fruit.

Kaş is a former fishing village, once inhabited by Greeks. Slightly crooked wooden houses with characteristic oriels line the picturesque old town alleyways, stone sarcophagi stand like memorials on the streets and tell the story of a long vanished ancient empire. The new Kaş is full of life. The old houses have become lively bars, small clubs and nice restaurants. Of course there are also a few shops selling tourist trinkets. Hamam towels here, jewelry there. And almost everywhere the well-known blue eye, the "nazar boncuğu", which promises happiness to the owner and protects him from evil eyes. It seems to work, at least Kaş was spared from being inundated by crowds of annoying tourist. But the main reason that Kas remains almost untouched, whose name means "eyebrow", is because it lies far away from the big hotels with hundreds and hundreds of beds like the area of Antalya, with its buffet battles and all-inclusive offers, in which some tourists calculate before their arrival how much beer they need to drink every day to get value for money.

Like almost every evening on this days in the late autumn of 2018, the conversations in Oxygen-Pub, which is only a stone's throw away from the jetties with the many yachts, are silenced at this time. The modern marina, completed only in 2013, is located at the end of a beautiful bay, sheltered by a miles-long peninsula that juts like a finger into the Mediterranean, and the mainland, which rises steeply to a low mountain range, the foothills of the Taurus Mountains in southern Turkey.

To landward at the top of the low mountain range, lies the "Sleeping Giant", a rugged rock so called by the inhabitants of the 9,000 soul town, that as the name suggests, looks as if there had been a giant lying down there and sleeping: head, shoulders and a massive body. On summer days, paragliders start in the mountains, circle Kaş on the warm ascending winds before landing on the quayside of the town harbor.

On this evening, as the day slowly gives way to the night, we look over the small headland towards Kastellorizo, the easternmost inhabited Greek island, so close to the Turkish coast, that you think you can swim effortlessly. We're all watching as the sun, once more heading towards the horizon, it looks like it's puffing itself up. Getting bigger and redder in an attempt to evade the inevitable daily plunge into the water. In the sky a thin veil of wispy clouds shine like flaming torches. The sea looks like it's on fire. Finally the sun gives up its desperate struggle and its fiery brilliance is extinguished once more.

Mark, the bald-headed South African with the distinctive laugh, orders the next round of beers. Glasses clink a toast to life, love and happiness. Dogs romp among the guests, who lounge on thick cushions on the gentle grassy slope in front of the bar. The blues singer tunes his guitar, his voice made distinctly throaty by one too many cigarettes. Then he plays his usual repertoire until late in the evening. Again another wonderful day has passed.

A stormy winter we spent together in Kaş. Until Spring. With the sun came the wanderlust. Some set the sails to circle the world. The others stayed. Another summer. Or the next one. Few of us have a concrete plan. That is what makes life so enjoyable. Even if our ways parted, friendships remained. And memories. Memories of the personal stories of ten sailors who all had the same dream - and the courage to implement it. Otherwise we would never have met.

There are Aannsha and Barry, two Australians who share a long and unusual love story. With sex, drugs and rock'n'roll on one hand and spiritual experiences on the other. They had to separate for over a decade before they found each other again. When the wanderlust seizes them, they sell their house and possessions, to sail the world. But there is just one problem: they have never sailed before.

There's Ismail, a young Turk who was arrested and sentenced after the Gezi protests in Istanbul. Disillusioned and frustrated by the politics of his homeland, he leaves the city - just like thousands of other well-educated Turks do at that time. However, he does not seek the freedom he longs for overseas. But on a sailboat. Since that moment he lives as a digital nomad on his 'Wanda'.

There are Clare and Zac. She's from Australia, he's from Alaska. In Florida they felt in love. Because a flight to Australia is too expensive, they buy a 40-year-old yacht,

refit it, and set sail. Destination: Down Under. But spontaneously they change course, cross the Atlantic and land in Europe. The reason: they are invited to a wedding.

There is Mark, a South African, who, after the death of his father, leaves South Africa to live in the Mediterranean Sea on board of his deceased father's yacht. At sea he finds what he has been seeking for so long, peace and tranquility, something he could not even find in Tibetan monasteries. The Turks call him "gülen amca", the smiling uncle.

There's Jim, a passionate nude art photographer, he sees his art as a tribute to God, whom he believes he encountered at a young age. After many personal and professional ups and downs in his life, his small business thrives in Scotland. But suddenly he thinks he has violated US export rules. In a touch of paranoia he already sees himself in a US jail. That's why he's preparing his escape. He wants to flee on a sail boat and settle in the Cape Verde Islands. But he has to learn to sail first.

There are Mike and Elaine. For twenty years, he works in construction to realise his big dream of circumnavigating the globe. In Elaine he finds a partner who supports him. But since the two Brits bought their 'Spicy Lady', they have hardly left Turkish waters. At least not on her own boat. To make their dream come true someday, the pair deliver yachts all over the Mediterranean.

And then there's me, a former business journalist. A complete burnout with anxiety and panic attacks which made me realize that I had to change everything. At that time my own mind caused me to be a virtual prisoner in my own apartment, unable to step outside the front door. Only the longing for a new and different life gave me the strength to make a radical change. In mid 2018 I quit my job, sold my apartment and bought a sail boat in Turkey. The sea is now my therapist.

During my breakdown, I discovered the videos of 'SV Delos'. The guys and girls around the Trautman brothers have been sailing around the world for almost ten years. One of the last professional articles I wrote was about the 'lifestyle business' of 'SV Delos'. And because the crew not only inspired me to my new life, but also others of our liveaboard group, they are also a part of this book. As a bonus chapter.

Each of us had arrived at this fork in life at which point we had to choose. Continue straight on, along the highway towards safety, pension and routine? Always straight, always concentrated, always full throttle. Unless one is slowed down. Or is in a traffic jam. Every day the same madness, the same distance to the '9-to-5-job', the same meetings, the same tasks, the same desks, the same colleagues.

A life as in three-quarter time. A waltz. A nice dance - but without much variety, a bit stiff, a bit old-fashioned. A clear step sequence. Clocked through as our life. You turn and turn and never stop. Until one gets dizzy. If you look in the faces of the Vienna Opera Ball, you may recognize a smile here and there, but rarely a laugh. One two Three. One two Three. Cannot make a mistake. No getting out of step. Do not miss a beat.

Or should you turn off the main highway of life, onto the unpaved and less travelled road? This beautiful avenue with the magnificent trees in bloom, where one does not know where it will end? A road with potholes which means you cannot race, but you can keep an eye on the untouched beauty of nature. At the next intersection the true adventure may already be waiting. Or a stunning view. Or the next party. This road is unpredictable. But full of joy.

We were dreamers.

Each of us dreamed of taking the turn on to this small enchanted road, longing for a new and different life. Some were deeply bored, the others stressed. Or just adventurous. Each of us still remembers the day we stood up with a head full of images of crystal clear water, white beaches, full sails and nights where a billion stars are strewn across the velvet blackness with even more dreams waiting to be born.

From these dreams reality was born, finally the decision to make life changes. To get out of everyday life as we knew it, to get off the mundane and immerse ourselves in a new world. Each of us was motivated by this step. This book tells the stories of those dreamers, those sailors, those with the courage to change their lives.

But it is not a sailing book in the true sense. It's not about saltwater-tainted captains boldly sharing their heroic deeds of rounding Cape Horn to an eager audience in the harbour bar. Rather, it is about people who enjoy their lives living on a yacht. Sailing is everyday life for them. So why talk about that? Many of our conversations which began with the words "I'm not really a good sailor", turned to stories of mishaps on the water, messed up docking maneuvers. Only incidentally did it emerge that some were on a circumnavigation of the world, others had already conquered the Atlantic Ocean or participated in sailing world championships.

'Dream on' tells the stories behind these sailors. The prehistory at the moment that changed their lives. It's about careful considerations, skepticism, courage and destinies. Dreaming on should not mean that one should continue to dream. Rather, it's about bringing the dream to life. To push it further. Make it bigger. Dreamlike is probably one of the words that fall most frequently from their mouths since leaving their old world behind. Be it a beautiful anchorage, an amazing sailing day, the ever changing water texture and colour, the sun rises and the sun sets, the friends, the food, the daily new experiences, the adventures. 'Dream on' is a guide to happiness.

This book is an attempt to stretch the question mark out straight until it becomes an exclamation point. To calm the fear, to awaken the child within and bring forth the natural curiosity about everything new and strange. Above all, however, this book is intended to do one thing: encourage a new chapter in your life. To give you a hunger for a life lived fully.

There are many excuses to stay in the routine of every-day life. Good excuses. Rational excuses. Job, family, pension. "I'd like to, but ...!", We often hear that. There are excuses. He who wants can also get. Albeit with the cuts that each of us had to make. You have to be ready for that. I remember one of the first days after I moved on board my 'Dilly-Dally'. I was moored in Marmaris. An older man, I think he was a Brit, stopped at the jetty in front of my boat. We chatted. I told him that I had quit my job, sold the apartment to live on my ship in the Mediterranean now. He looked at me, asked about my age. "46," I replied. He nodded, raising his hand in farewell. As he wandered away with a curved back, he re-minded me of Colombo. He stopped and turned around. "Everything's perfectly timed!" He said. "You know, I worked all my life and my dream was to live on a yacht, to travel the world." Every year, he postponed the plan. Now he has his yacht, but he is too old to enjoy it. He's no longer capable of long passages. "Next year me and my wife will spend some time on a cruise ship," he said. "To at least see some of the places I wanted to sail to." He gave me a thumbs up, turned and left.

Life on a sailboat is not always pleasant. It is above all a restriction, a renunciation of luxury. Even in the Medi-terranean. The winters are cold and stormy. If you want to live on a boat, you have to be willing to limit yourself, you have to accept that not everything will go to plan. That no week passes without repairs, even if they are small or unexpectedly big. Therefore, a decision should not be made blue-eyed on a whim. And it should be well calculated. As low as the cost of living may be, if you don't have cash on hand for repairs and maintenance, your dream will fail.

If you keep your costs down, depending on the area you're sailing and avoiding expensive marinas, you can live well on 500 Euros a month. In addition, however, comes the maintenance of the boat. A rule of thumb is that at least 1.5 percent of the value should be reserved monthly. A sailboat is not comparable to a motorhome. In case of damage on the high seas, you can't pull over to the side of the road and wait for the breakdown vehicle. Those who invest in their ship invest in their safety.

On the other hand you do not have to be rich to fulfill the dream of life on board. Almost everywhere there are opportunities to create an income. Everyone has hidden talents that they can bring forth. Even if many have not recognized it yet.

We became friends.

We celebrated Christmas together, danced into the new year. Far from home, but without homesickness. When the winter storms whipped waves into Kaş harbour and gale-force wind gusts wrecked biminis, sails and solar panels in the marina, we spent time together sharing meals on our floating homes. The torrential rain sounded like an army marching across the deck, the mooring lines creaked and groaned, the wind shrieked through the rigging and we counted the seconds between the lightning and the thunder to judge if the storm was getting closer or further away.

We all lived a similar life. But have now stepped out of the everyday life. Some have been sailing since childhood, others have bought a boat without much experience. On these long cold winter evenings as we ate, drank and laughed, each one of us warmed as we shared our unique stories of how we ended up living on our yachts in this strange beautiful place called Kaş.

If you can find something, in one or all of these stories, that resonates with you or if this book inspires even one person to change their life, then it has done its job. It does not matter if the trip leads to the sea, to a lake house or to the mountains.

Dream On!

WET GRAY NOMADS

AANNSHA & BARRY

abs

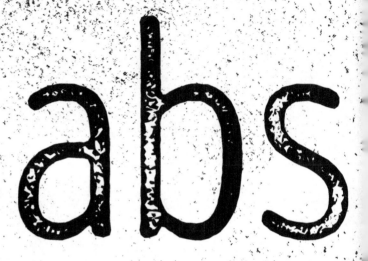

AANNSHA
58, AUSTRALIA

BARRY
56, AUSTRALIA

MISSION: circumnavigating the globe

BUDGET: limited

SCHEDULE: unlimited

FINANCED BY: Youtube & Patreon

Aannsha and Barry's story is about painful separations, spiritual experiences, sex, drugs & rock'n'roll and bizarre dreams. Above all, it is about a great love between two freedom-loving souls who take twelve years to finally find themselves. And when they finally lead an orderly life, they throw everything overboard, which promises financial security, quit their jobs, sell their house and sail on a sailboat - without ever previously sailed.

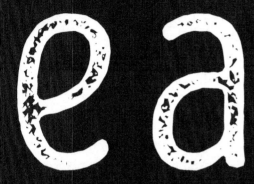

BUILT: 1994
BOUGHT: 2018
PRICE: 75.000 €

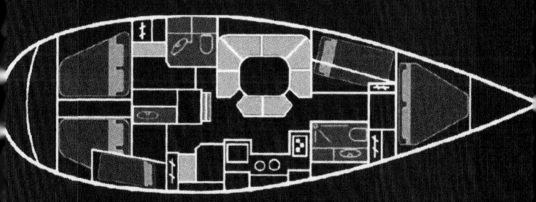

SUN ODYSSEY 45.1
length: 14,15m, beam: 4,48m, draft: 2,00m

AB Sea is created from the initial letters of Aannsha and Barry. As neither of both had ever set foot on a yacht prior to learning to sail in February 2018 it was like going back to school (ABC). To give the name a nautical twist they changed C to Sea.

The story of Aannsha, then known as Rebecca, and Barry could have been ordinary and predictable: two young bank clerks, she is 21years old, he is two years younger. They get acquainted during further education classes, fall in love, buy one of those pretty stone houses that are typical in the northwest of England, on the Wirral peninsula just south of Liverpool and fall into the routine of life. The rhythm of their lives revolve around bank office hours. After work they go to the pub, walk in the park or sit on the sofa watching TV. Holidays are always to the same hotel, because it's so beautiful there, because they know people there. That's how it goes until retirement and a pension. The end.

But the story of Aannsha and Barry is different. Completely different. It leads first from England via France, the USA and Tenerife to Australia. It is about painful separations, failed marriages, spiritual experiences, sex, drugs & rock'n'roll, music and art and bizarre dreams. Above all, it is about a great love between two freedom-loving souls who take twelve years to finally find themselves. And when they finally find themselves, they do, for a while, lead an ordinary life on the east coast of Australia. When their son grows up and moves out of the family home, they decide on a radical lifestyle change. Shunning financial security they quit their jobs, sell their house and possessions and buy a sailboat - without ever having previously sailed.

With this they fulfill their dream. In truth it's actually his dream. But Aannsha does not want to live life without Baz. „I feel younger every day," says the 58-year-old after her first year at sea. At first she had doubts. The sea scared her. Being cooped up in a tiny boat in endless blue space. The unpredictable. The unknown. Wind and weather. No calculable factors. Certainly not for someone who had never spent a night on a boat in their life. „Actually, I'm more of a cautious type," says Aannsha. „But I've overcome a lot of my self-doubt and become much more confident over the past year." She smiles with satisfaction. „That's a great feeling."

Since April 2018, the couple who have dual UK and Australian citizenship have lived full time on board „AB Sea"; they do not have any other home. They crossed the Mediterranean from west to east sailing from Spain to Turkey. One day they want to sail their home back to Australia. First across the Atlantic, then the Pacific. Maybe in ten or even fifteen years. For a beer with old friends. And then? Then it should go on. To wherever.

When Aannsha sees Barry for the first time, she works at a bank. She is a young, beautiful woman, after which men inevitably turn around. She has long dark blond hair and dresses sexily. Short skirts and figure hugging tops. But Aannsha does not feel content in the 9 to 5 world. Money has never meant anything to her. Since her youth, she paints, muses on life, has a penchant for the supernatural. The decision to work for a bank was a logical one. „Do something sensible," her mind dictated. She knew her family was hoping for a solid career path for her. But she really wanted to follow her dreams.

At that time, the beginning of the 80s, at a college banking class, she immediately noticed the attractive guy with dark hair: Barry, or as his friends call him: Baz. He looks good, no doubt about that, but something makes him special. „It was his walk," remembers Aannsha. Her eyes sparkle when she thinks of the time almost 40 years ago. „Baz stalked like a tiger. Majestic. Confident. Somehow sublime".

During a lunch break, the two speak for the first time. Not about banking or careers. They talk about music. The era of disco, soul and funk is coming to an end, pop bands like the Human League, Roxy Music, U2 and Blondie are conquering the charts. Since Barry was 15 years old, he'd been a part time DJ. He sees his future as a full time DJ, certainly not behind the counter of a bank. When he hears that Aannsha works for the TSB, a British private and commercial bank, he laughs aloud. Doesn't TSB stand for „try something better?" he asks. That's exactly what he's looking for. Something better.

Aannsha admires Barry. He has dreams, but he is not a dreamer. He has a clear plan for his career as a DJ. Barry heard of a place near Saint Tropez where he could get DJ work. He wants to go there, with an old VW LT 31 van and some good friends. The bank career? Pah! That impresses Aannsha. She loves how Barry approaches life and very soon she loves him too. He was fascinated by Aannsha from the very first minute.

The two become a couple, forge plans together and finally resign from their jobs at the bank. The time had come to set off for the south of France. On board: Barry's mobile disco equipment, thousands of vinyl records and Aannsha's art materials. The pinch: Unemployment is rampant in the UK. For the first time, more than a million people have no job. In such unsteady times you don't quit a well paying career! Barry and Aannsha do not care.

The hoped for dream jobs in France fails at the French customs. They believe Barry wants to sell his records and the disco equipment illegally. They have to turn back, document every single record in England and fill in the appropriate papers. Name of the record, artist, label, price. For three days, the two work together to type very long lists. When they finally get to the south of France, Barry has missed his first work opportunity.

Eventually he gets a job as a DJ on a campsite near Port Grimaud in the south of France. Aannsha sells some of her paintings. To increase their budget, they help out at the campsite, sharing a caravan with four other temporary workers. Not the best choice for a young couple in love. When the fridge is suddenly full of face cream and other cosmetics and Barry can't find space for his beer, they move into a tent. After nine months and a summer full of unforgotten moments, they return to England.

Barry's father is tired of his son wasting his time with idiotic DJ plans. He gives him work in his manufacturing business and hopes his son will one day take over from him. Barry's dreamer life must finally come to an end. To further bind him, Barry's father helps them to buy a house. „That's a good investment," he advises his son. For once Barry listens to his father's advice. Together with Aannsha, who has found a job as a secretary, they are back on the 9 to 5 treadmill and now paying a mortgage.

On the weekends Barry still works as a DJ in the local clubs. Aannsha mixes drinks, dances in short skirts and fishnet tights on the counter. Barry is getting closer to his dream of becoming a well-known DJ. Aannsha begins to feel empty. Only a few days at first, then more often. She wonders about the meaning in her life. Only working and partying, surely that can't be all there is? She does not know where she wants to go. What she wants. She's hoping for dialogue with Barry about how she feels, but he's making the playlist for his next DJ gig. Aannsha's head and heart are beginning to clash. This cannot go well.

They love each other, they argue, they reconcile. Barry's life runs in a straight line, Aannsha's unsure of her direction. She's craving his attention. Aannsha gets her hairdresser sister to cut her hair short and dye it platinum blonde, a bit like Marilyn Monroe. She feels great. When Barry sees her, he tells her, „What the hell? What did you do with your hair?" She cries, he does not even see the tears. His eyes are fixed on his career as a DJ.

The attention that Aannsha misses from Barry, she finds with a colleague behind the bar at the club. It's a fatal kiss that destroys their relationship. Barry, who is aware of the breach of trust confronts Aannsha. „What are you going to do now?" He asks angrily. She knows no other answer than „I'll leave you!"

Aannsha believes she has crossed the line with the kiss. After two and a half years together, the two go their separate ways. Aannsha signs her half of the house over to Barry and moves out only with her personal belongings. She is ashamed to have cheated on him. Even if it was just a kiss.

Back living with her mother, Aannsha tries to forget about Barry, erasing him from her life. She plunges into the next relationship, marrying hastily. But even without contact Barry is always there, somehow. Aannsha's marriage lasts only two years.

Aannsha always had a penchant for the spiritual. As a child, she dreamed that her father would die, and shortly afterwards he was dead. Since then, she tries to interpret dreams, is convinced that there is more between heaven and earth than most people believe. Forces, influences, energies that influence us.

She embarks on a meditative journey, is passionate about the transcendent, dream interpretation and tarot. During this time, Rebecca the girl from Wirral, transforms to become Aannsha the shaman. She attends seminars, finds mentors, travels through England, Greece and California in search of herself and meets an Australian at a rainbow festival. She believes she has finally found the great love, a man with whom she can talk about everything she understands and wants to understand. She moves with him to Australia and later becomes an Australian citizen. Maybe here, on the other side of the world, she can finally forget Barry. Aannsha still has occasional contact with his mother. From her she learns that he ended up in Tenerife Canary Islands, working full time as a professional DJ.

After separating from Aannsha, Barry focuses on his career as a DJ. The job with his father annoys him. Music and women are his new life content. Hook up, have fun, accelerate. Not only in the clubs but also at the wheel. One night, Barry crashes into a tree. He is drunk. He gets away with some minor injuries, but the car is a write off and he loses his driving license for twelve months. Without a car it is impossible for him to drive to his DJ gigs. Barry searches for alternatives and makes contact with an old friend who lives in Tenerife.

The British are conquering the Island, Tenerife is the Mecca of party tourism. As a DJ, his buddy tells him, there's a good chance of getting a job there. Barry does not have to think twice. He spontaneously leaves his home country to start a new life in the Canary Islands. It does not take long for Barry to meet a new lady friend, a Spaniard from an influential family. Similar to Aannsha, the wedding bells ring soon. Barry is now an islander, his new relationship is a license to Tenerife. Baz is back!

At night Barry works the holidaymakers into a frenzy in several different clubs. He calls himself „Barry Noble". He is a local star DJ. With a Spanish colleague, he starts a radio program called Spanglish Showtime, which means that it's presented in English and in Spanish, depending on who is currently at the microphone. A little later Barry founded the first 24 hour English-language radio station on the island, presenting his own show and managing the station. The 80's and 90's are good to him. There is no room for a jealous wife and especially not the frowning in-laws. As hastily as the wedding came, the divorce ensued. His life now consists of sex, drugs & rock'n'roll.

Barry thinks he has arrived at Olympus. A string of female tourists end up in his bed. In 1987 he publishes the „Condom Rap Tenerife". In the song Barry raps to the tune of „Relax" by Frankie goes to Hollywood about protected intercourse. An AIDS awareness song he calls it. His female fans see this more as an invitation to sex, which he willingly accepts. The song can still be found on YouTube. The video is a smorgasbord of quirky photos. Always in the picture: Barry. Sometimes in garish 80s clothes, sometimes with a hair style which would make Jon Bon Jovi blush, sometimes with beer cans on his head, from which straws extend to his mouth. Or half naked in the whirlpool. Always laughing, always partying, always a drink in hand. At night he becomes an animal, then he is back, the tiger ready to hunt. Every hedonistic delight is on the table. But in the afternoons, when he awakes in his apartment with a headache, lies alone in bed, or thinks about how to get rid of the woman next to him, he often thinks of Aannsha, his great love. How is she? What's she doing now?

Each of them tried to forget the other in their own way. Without success. Aannsha had gone on a journey to find herself and the meaning of life, Barry vowed to distract himself with non-stop partying. „I was a huge asshole" he says today, „But I wouldn't change anything I did during that time…".

The parties in Tenerife are getting wild. Barry refuses to see that he physically and psychologically suffers from the lifestyle. He ignores that. Then Barry is about to collapse. After more than ten years of party, excesses and fame, he begins to rethink his life. He feels the emptiness inside him. For eleven months he renounces alcohol, women and wild parties, concentrating more and more on his career as a radio presenter. The people he considered his friends no longer want to hang out with the new boring Barry. Who wants a party animal for a friend who does not party hard anymore?

At this time, it is May 1996 and on the other side of the globe Aannsha has a confused dream. Yet again. It feels as real as it did when she dreamt of her father dying. This time it's about Barry. She senses that he needs her help. She calls his mother, tells of her dream. She's given Barry's phone number in Tenerife. It's been 12 years since they last spoke. After a couple of stiff drinks with friends, Aannsha goes home and makes the call to the Canary Islands. It rings. Once, twice, three times.

It's late morning in Tenerife. For Barry that's still the middle of the night. „Who the hell is calling me at this time of the day?" he thinks, angry at the call, angry at his life. He moulds the pillow around his ears. Then finally the answering machine picks up. „Hello it's Aannsha here … You may remember me as Rebecca …" Barry does not need to hear any more. He recognized her voice at the first word. He rushes to pick up the phone.

Aannsha has been single again for 18 months. For seven years she and the Australian guy were a couple. She now works as an assistant in a government department, paints again in her spare time and still asks herself the questions to which she did not find any answers in her mid-20s. What is the meaning of your life? Why do your relationships never go anywhere? Why can't she get Barry out of her head? They'd had no communication with each other for 12 years.

When her last relationship fell apart, Aannsha made a list. Both sides of an A4 sheet full of features that Mr. Right needed to bring along to a new relationship. It's a lot about feelings. To the attitude to life. Listening and trust. How to tackle problems together and then solve them. It's also about children. Actually she had never wanted children. Barry, neither. Aannsha includes in the list trivial things, things like: The man who can make her happy must have read John Gray's „Men are from Mars, Women are from Venus," a relationship book about why men often have such a hard time understanding women. And vice versa.

The first telephone call, after twelve years of silence between them, lasts hours. The next day they call, and the day after. And if they do not talk on the phone, they write heartfelt and deep, pagelong letters. This is how it goes for weeks and months. In the autumn, when Aannsha is visiting England, Barry invites her to come to Tenerife for a week. He pays for her flight and picks her up at the airport. Aannsha hopes to bring a closing conclusion to the chapter of "Barry" with her visit. One last meeting, a final discussion. She wants to let him go. The exact opposite happens.

The first thing Barry needs to say to Aannsha at the airport is that he is sorry for what he said about her hairstyle. At that time, just before the breakup. The Marilyn-Monroe cut was good for her, he says. She's amazed that he can remember it. And then, on the drive to Barry's villa, which is a short fifteen minutes, Barry does not stop talking. He, who always shied away from long conversations, talks without pause almost to the point of babbling. "It was like a movie," says Aannsha. "He said all the things that I thought he would not care about or remember." On the short drive, they talk about everything that has accumulated in twelve years. Even about children. And getting married. When they arrive at his villa, there is a book on his bedside table: "Men are from Mars, women are from Venus". They will get to know each other again this week. This time differently. And reignite their love for each other.

When Aannsha gets on the plane after seven days, she is pregnant. He must come to Australia, she says on the phone later when she tells him about the pregnancy. Tenerife is not the place where our child should grow up. Barry does not hesitate a second. He sells his beloved record collection, far below value, and books the next flight. On Valentine's Day 1998, the two marry. They have no money for a party, so each of the guests brings something to the party. You have to improvise. „It was a great party," says Aannsha. Completely informal and relaxed. Like her life. On October 21, 1998, her son is born. They call him Luke. A new era begins.

With Barry's DJ career now over and the wild lifestyle a distant memory. He is now quite the faithful and loving father of a family. But he is struggling in Australia. Only when he is accepted as a „resident" he may officially work. He applies for radio jobs as a presenter, but his British accent plays against him. So he works as a copywriter for commercials and radio station ID's. That does not bring him fulfillment. After 5 years, and now an Australian citizen, he resigns from that job. Their neighbour has a bus company and Barry gets a bus driver's license and then brings children to and from school for two years. But a school bus driver is not his dream job either.

Because he is good at fixing computers, he buys an IT repair company. A franchise model. He works a lot, earns little. Franchise fees are too high. He dumps the franchise and goes independent. His clients are mostly older people who don't understand their computer. The widow who is afraid she'll delete the Internet. The senior, who says firmly that he didn't do anything, the computer is just broken.

Barry makes home visits, helps, explains, services, and repairs only when it really needs to be done. He keeps his pricing low, because his customers usually have only a little pension money. He often brings home cakes, homemade jams and vegetables as a form of payment. Aannsha also changes her job several times. Earning a living, that's all. She does not really enjoy work, has no passion. But the two have dedication and responsibility. For Luke. So they keep at it day after day.

The three lead a modest life in Australia, living in a small house on the east coast, but it is their sanctuary. They see their son grow up, the child of their love. That makes them happy. And yet deep down things are rumbling. Especially within Barry. Aannsha has changed her job again, she is now working for a small family business. For the first time in her life, she goes to work relaxed, having fun. Luke is now grown up. And then Barry makes a wild and crazy proposition, to which Aannsha has only one answer: „No! No way! Absolutely not!" Their relationship abruptly comes to a decision point.

It's August 31st 2016 when the seed is planted into Barry's mind. He spends a short vacation on the Gold Coast in Queensland with Aannsha. On Sunday, they visit an old friend who has just bought a brand new motor yacht. A roaring beast. A Four Winns 318, 33 feet long, equipped with a 600 hp power package in the engine room. They jet along the coast, anchor in front of small beaches, drink beer and have a fabulous day. Barry is excited. In the car, on the way back to the hotel, he begins to muse. What if they also bought a small boat? Barry is an experienced scuba diver with over 300 dives. With the boat he could reach remote dive spots.

The dream bursts a day later when returning to reality. Bills pile up on the kitchen counter. Financial reserves: not a lot there! Disappointed and distracted, Barry searches for diving videos on YouTube. He finds the video „Sailing the Great Barrier Reef". A few young guys and girls sailing around the world, they dive at the most gorgeous spots on the globe and just have a good time. Barry is looking for more videos. And is astonished. At the time he discovers their channel, the crew of „SV Delos" had put more than 180 films on YouTube. Sharing their adventurous lives on the water, they can apparently also fund their adventure through YouTube. Barry binge watches all of their videos. If they can, why not him and Aannsha? An idea was born.

He has often talked to Aannsha about what they will do when their son moves out of the house. For both it is clear that they would like to see something of the world. Now that Luke is 18 years old and wants to move to Brisbane, decision day is getting closer. So one evening Barry poses the question that has been bothering him for a long time: „What do you think if we sell everything here and sail around the world?" He had expected a clear „yes!", not such a brusque and absolute rejection.

Barry's proposal will be a test of their marriage. Aannsha thinks he's just dreaming. Barry seriously says, „If you don't come with me, then I'll do it on my own." Then desolately says „I have to do something, this life is killing me. I'm dying on the inside." Amazingly, it's Luke who acts as a mediator between the two. Barry, the head man, the planner, the structured person, has thought through everything several times. And the more he tells and explains, with passion and love, the more Aannsha gives the crazy idea a chance. The idea of exploring the world on a yacht pleases her more and more. Even if she has never been on a sailing yacht.

But how should they finance the adventure? Can they even afford to buy a boat in their fifties, far from the pension? Without reserves, without a plan, how will they make an income? There are no definitive answers to these questions. But they know that their resolve is not determined by a cash reward, but instead with infinite freedom, many adventures and unforgettable moments. That, they decide, is worth the risk.

First, they are interested in a catamaran. But a double-hull is out of their budget range, even if they can sell their home for a good price, plus the cars and all their belongings. So the search is refined to only monohulls, modern yachts that meet their needs: the boat must be stable and safe enough to sail all over the world's oceans. It also has to provide enough space because the ship will be their only home in the future. It must be easy to use by two people. And it must not blow the budget. That's the sticking point.

The choices are quickly reduced. Too expensive. Too old. Too ugly. Too poorly equipped. Too many cabins. Months pass with the search on the Internet. At the same time, the two renovate their house with friends help in order to sell it at the highest possible price. After three months, the house and garden are sparkling and look amazing. At the beginning of October 2017, a realtor will offer the property. To the viewing come quite a few interested parties, who submit their offers. Two days later, the purchase contract is signed. There is no going back. They have exactly 35 days left to move out. They sell everything that does not fit in four suitcases, each weighing just 23 kilograms. Their whole lives reduced to a small pile of bags.

The plan is to fly first to Spain, where Barry's brother has an apartment that they can stay in. From there they want to visit the boats that have aroused their interest. Buying a yacht in Australia is out of the question for them. Comparable boats cost in their home country are about 30,000 Euros more than the Mediterranean. But before the adventure can really begin, there is another little thing to do: they must first learn to sail. And from the bottom up. Their basic sailing knowledge: 0!

In February 2018 they drive to Gibraltar. Here they spend 17 days taking sailing lessons, gain initial experience, test whether they are even seaworthy or already seasick in the harbour. They learn to tie knots, all about seamanship, navigation and meteorology. Lots of theory and even more sailing terms. And then it starts. Out onto the sea they go. Barry is excited. The first time he is at the helm, steering the yacht. He seeks the wind, sets the sails and feels the power that goes through the boat. As it picks up speed, cuts through the clear water, soundless but powerful. How to become one with the sea. Only driven by the wind. „That's when I knew we'd made the right decision," says Barry. „I'd never felt so alive."

Aannsha still has to overcome some fears. „I'm a coward by nature," she says. And she is all the more surprised when, during a force eight gale, she volunteers to reef the mainsail. She goes forward to the mast, cranks on the winch with all her might, pushing and flaking the sail -

and then it's done. „When the sail was reefed, I looked around, saw the metres-high waves, felt the wind in my face. But I wasn't afraid! I was so elated," says Aannsha.

Two months later on the east coast of Spain they buy their yacht. For weeks they had viewed yachts, compared and negotiated. And now the reality was they had found their dream yacht: a Jeanneau Sun Odyssey 45.1, built in 1995 and very well maintained. Weeks before they had visited this yacht, but then the deal had failed at different price expectations. Now the seller has agreed to: 75,000 Euros. The ink at the bottom of the contract is quickly dry.

Aannsha and Barry spend three months in the marina, putting additional equipment on the yacht to suit their needs, waiting and caring, getting used to life in a small, constantly moving space. In August they leave the marina, sail to the Balearic Islands and back again. A shake down sail. There are just a few minor tweaks when they return to the marina.

Then the adventure really begins as they set off on the long passage east through the Mediterranean to Turkey with two friends who come on board: Mike and Elaine, two experienced sailors. Barry knows Mike from his days as a DJ in Tenerife. Mike also worked there in the clubs. Mike and Elaine have lived on a sailboat in Kaş for five years. And that's also Aannsha and Barry's first goal. Turkey, where they want to spend the winter. When they arrive, the seas have given them experience and confidence, both in themselves and their yacht and home called A B Sea. Since leaving their old lives, they have not regretted a day - despite small setbacks here and there, these things are always present in any lifestyle.

They enjoy every day. They do not miss their old home in Australia. Only their son.

The days of life go by. Finding new friends. Experiencing new vistas. And also with work. Since the budget is tight, Aannsha and Barry try to keep their costs as low as possible. They avoid expensive marinas, preferring to tie up in cheaper town harbours. Ideally, they will anchor. Only in winter, anchoring is not possible. The weather is too unpredictable, the storms too violent, the thunderstorms too powerful.

With their new and very different lifestyle they document everything, the good, the bad and the ugly in their weekly videos and blog posts, just as Barry has seen „SV Delos" do it. Every Friday two new blogs appear on the website, written by Aannsha and Barry in a kind of his and hers viewpoint. On Saturdays a video, usually around 15 minutes long, is posted on YouTube. Their fan base on YouTube is growing and after only a few months small amounts of money come trickling in from the YouTube adverts.

On Patreon, a kind of crowd funding platform on the Internet, they are also supported by some faithful and enthusiastic viewers, who pay a small fee for each video they produce. Their patrons want to see this couple succeed and continue to document their lives as they explore foreign cultures and cities, learn a little more every day about sailing and share the ups and downs. Aannsha, who lives out her passion for art, paints pictures and makes jewellery that she sells.

The next one or two years, they will travel the Mediterranean gaining more sailing experience. Then it's through the Strait of Gibraltar on to the Canary Islands, from there with a stopover on the Cape Verde across the Atlantic to Brazil. „We're planning a few years for the Caribbean," says Barry. Then they'll find their way through the Panama Canal to South America, from there across the Pacific to the Solomon Islands. After a flying visit to Australia they want to continue. First to Indonesia and then to the Maldives.

And then? „Let's see, that's just the plan for the next ten to fifteen years," Barry says and laughs. There is no plan B for retirement or anything like that. Everything they own is on board their floating home A B Sea.

And so they feel like nomads at sea. „Gray nomads" are what they call retirees in Australia who travel the world. Aannsha and Barry proudly call themselves „wet gray nomads": Even if they are far from being retired.

If you want to follow the adventures of Aannsha and Barry, check their website www.absea.com.au. Or follow ‚AB Sea" on Instagram, Facebook or Youtube: @sailingabsea

ISMAIL

THE
REBEL

BUILT: 2001
BOUGHT: 2016
PRICE: 80.000€

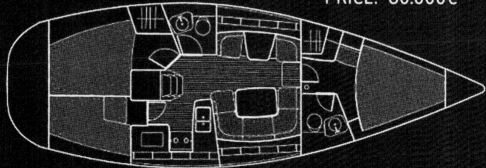

SUN ODYSSEY 40 DS
length: 12,2m, beam: 3,95m, draft: 1,95m

As a travel entrepreneur Ismail's work takes him to many places and sitting in a restaurant called ,Wanda' in Dubrovnik, Croatia, he thinks that would be a great name for a yacht. When he finally buys his boat to live on, that's what he names her ,Wanda' - the wanderer.

- THE WANDERER-

40, TURKEY

PROFESSION: Tourism

PASSION: Globetrotter

PANIC: Claustrophobia

ISMAIL

At the Gezi protests in Istanbul Ismail is arrested and later sentenced. The young Turk loses faith in democracy in his homeland and decides to leave Istanbul. But where will he go? A sailboat, he believes, offers him the greatest possible freedom. First Ismail wants to sail the Mediterranean, then the oceans of the world.

On the evening that Ismail loses his belief in democracy in his homeland, he's sitting on a bus with friends and acquaintances travelling through Istanbul. A wonderfully warm early summer's day is ending, just as the sun is shining over the Bosphorus, leaving long pointed shadows just like spears from the hundreds of minarets in the city, onto the streets of old Constantinople. Like the previous day, Ismail, has spent today in the park in his neighborhood. A small park, not far from the striking Taksim Square, where the famous shopping street Istiklal ends with the historic tram. Ever since he moved back to Istanbul, Ismail regularly visits this park and walks his dog, which he rescued from the dusty streets of the metropolis and nursed to full health.

For a few days now, he's been spending the night with friends in the park. In the afternoon they would sit together, sing to the sounds of guitars, meditate, play or just lay in the shade in the meadow among the few trees and read. In the juggernaut-mile of Istanbul, in hot summer months, when the asphalts glow and the air flickers, the park is an oasis of relaxation. The Istanbulers love their park, which was opened in 1869 as the first public park in the Ottoman capital. But the world has only known about the park since late May / early June 2013 when it was the site of fervent demonstrations. Almost exactly when Ismail is sitting in this bus. The park in question is called Gezi. And the bus is on its way to the police headquarters. It is a prisoner van.

On this evening of June 3, tear gas wafts like thick ground fog over the sparse green in Gezi Park; people are violently dispersed. The streets of Istanbul look like a war zone. Barricades are being built, car tires are burning. Protesters try to stop the oncoming police, who want to bludgeon the protest with all severity. Mosques become emergency hospitals. But the police can not be stopped. Again and again small groups of demonstrators are isolated and then arrested. Including Ismail – as are 254 other people on this fateful evening.

Ismail, then in his mid-30s, is detained at the police station for several days. He is being penned in a cell with other demonstrators. There may be 15 or even 20, including some foreigners. Ismail translates for them. The authorities accuse him of being one of the organizers of the Gezi protests. He shakes his head. „That's nonsense. There were no organizers. We demonstrated against the clearing of the park. That's all. We were just environmentalists, neighborhood residents who oppose the construction companies."

Spontaneous action begun by a few dozen environmental activists as the diggers move in to level the park for construction of a new shopping mall, is developing its own momentum, plunging Turkey into a deep crisis. More and more citizens join the protests. First hundreds, then thousands, then hundreds of thousands - in Istanbul alone. When the protests have long been conquered by politics, the wave of indignation spills over the whole of Turkey. A conflagration. In 80 of the country's 81 provinces, 3.5 million people hit the streets. This is the number that has been published by the Turkish Ministry of Interior. It's probably even more.

Today's Turkish President Recep Tayyip Erdoğan, then Prime Minister, insults the men, women and children who take part in the demonstrations as „rats" and „terrorists" and allows a crack down on them. The bloody record: nine dead and 8163 injured. Tear gas, water cannons and rubber bullets are used, several demonstrators lose their eyesight. Rest will not come until the security forces finally clear the Gezi Park on 15 June.

Of the 255 arrested this evening in early June, 82 are convicted. One of them is Ismail, who has never seen himself as a political person. The process begins on the 23rd of December. The Turkish media characterise the term „255 from Gezi Park". An Istanbul court sentences Ismail to five years in prison for something called „violation of the right of assembly". What the exact reason was, Ismail cannot remember. For him, the verdict is a farce anyway. However, he doesn't have to go to prison, his sentence is a suspended sentence with a good behaviour bond.

Nevertheless, Ismail appeals against the verdict. From today's perspective, it's a mistake. Had he accepted the suspended sentence, his good behaviour period would now be over. But accepting the verdict was out of the question for him. However the process for this new appeal is still pending and his good behaviour period only starts once the verdict and sentence are confirmed. Should Ismail become „conspicuous" in the meantime, he will be jailed immediately.

To prevent this, Ismail decides to move. At least out of Istanbul. „Gezi was the last chance for democracy in Turkey," Ismail says, disillusioned. „It died with the suppression of the protests." When the mayoral election in Istanbul in May 2019 is annulled after the opposition candidates win by a fine margin, Ismail sees that his assessment has been confirmed.

Immediately after the verdict however in 2013, Ismail feels confined in Istanbul. But he doesn't want to go abroad, where he lived for many years earlier. He loves his Istanbul home and misses her. That's why he returned - just before the protests.

In November 1978 Ismail was born in Ankara, the Turkish capital. His father makes his career in the government, Ismail and his brother, who works as a pilot today, have a privileged upbringing. When Ismail is twelve years old, the family moves to the Netherlands for four years. His father works in the diplomatic service at the Turkish embassy. The children attend international schools, learning English and Dutch. Back in Turkey and after leaving school Ismail moves to Istanbul to study, living a casual life. He lives in a student flat share in Beşiktaş. He occasionally goes sailing with friends on the Bosporus and the Sea of Marmara. He enjoys the hours when he can escape the hustle and bustle of the big city. But he doesn't suspect that he will one day live on a sailboat.

Ismail is studying International Relations and Political Science with limited interest. He is still young and doesn't know what to do with his life. By choosing these subjects, he believes he is doing what his father wants. On the other hand, his job as a white water rafting guide is much more fun.

He provides an adrenaline rush for summer tourists in the wild rivers of the Taurus Mountains near Antalya. His language skills make him a coveted guide. For

tourists in Turkey, but also for Turks abroad. He begins to accompany Turkish tour groups to Europe more and more often. After two years he packs in his studies. He earns good money in tourism and also sees the world. He finds hanging out in lecture halls a mere waste of time.

He lives in Egypt for one year, organising Nile cruises. In 2010 he moves to Dubrovnik in Croatia. The Balkans are popular with Turks, after all the lands once belonged to the Ottoman Empire. Ismail realizes the potential. Turkey is booming economically, and instead of vacations to relatives, more and more Turks spend their holidays abroad. Ismail founds the first Turkish travel provider for Eastern Europe. He calls his company Eastwest Travel. For Europeans, the region is in the east, for the Turks it is in the west. He serves both groups. After three years in Dubrovnik however, his yearning for his homeland is growing. He leaves Croatia and moves back to Istanbul. He opens an office near Gezi Park. And he's one of the first environmental activists to stand up to bulldozers when they roll in. He spends every day in the park now. Until his arrest.

Istanbul is choking him with frustration and disappointment. He leaves the city which he's just returned to, in order to find somewhere he can continue his impressively developing business. Like Ismail, many young, well-educated Istanbulers are doing the same thing. After the Gezi protests, around 200,000 people leave the city, most of them go abroad.

Ismail however, goes to Datça, which is idyllically situated west of Marmaris on the Mediterranean coast. His parents have a summer house there. First, he considers building a small facility for young, creative backpackers with studio accomodation. He's gained enough inspiration for these on his trips around the world. But he's lost his confidence in the state. He figures he either won't get permission, or his project will be copied. Or else it'll be misappropriated because some official's relative suddenly holds a document in his hand stating that the property belongs to him. In Turkey, says Ismail, you have to expect everything.

After the recent experiences in Istanbul, Ismail really only wants one thing: freedom and peace! And he believes he can best find that on a sailing boat. He often spends the evenings in Datça, in „Coop Bar", his home away from home right by the pier, where many yachts moor. That inspires him. The operators become his friends and so Ismail is now not only a fan of sailing ships, but also a German football club - the FC Sankt Pauli.

The bar owner who lived for some time in the Port of Hamburg, never misses a game of his favorite club on television. Several times a year he flies to the club's home matches at the Millerntor stadion. Actually Ismail is a Beşiktaş fan, but the ideals of the FC Sankt Pauli, a left-wing club mostly playing in the second football league in Germany, impress him: Tolerant and cosmopolitan. No to racism! Yes to multiculturalism!

The idea of living on a boat gets stuck in Ismail's head. He would be independent, but never have to move house. If he gets bored in one place, he can set sail and anchor elsewhere. He also loves traveling. To circum-navigate the world on a ship is a childhood dream. But first, the Mediterranean is enough. He's earned good money with his travel agency and built a network of agents on the ground. He can reach the contacts he cultivates from anywhere in the world. Sometimes Ismail sits in front of his computer all day, sometimes just for two hours. All he needs to do his job is an internet connection.

Ismail is visiting friends in Dubrovnik when he decides to continue his business on the water. He meets them in the evening, eating in his favorite restaurant. It's called „Wanda". Wouldn't that be a fitting name for his sailing vessel? „Wanda - the wanderer". A tribute to his life as a globetrotter. But first Ismail has to overcome a small hurdle. His sailing skills are rusty. He hasn't been on the water since he began university.

Back in Turkey, Ismail contacts his old friend Kıvanç Sevinç, a top Turkish sailor who participates in the TP52-world series for the Turkish team Provezza. There, Sevinç sails with 2003 America's Cup winner Peter Holmberg, who once led the Alinghi to victory. One stormy winter, Sevinç and Ismail cruise between Istanbul's Kalamış Marina and the Princes' Islands daily for a fortnight on his friend's training boat, a Jeanneau 24. So Ismail learns from one of Turkey's best sailors everything he needs to know about sailing and also about his future life on a boat.

Ismail, an avid motorcycling fan, drives his bike along the coast, starting in Çanakkale in the Dardanelles where the Mediterranean kisses the Sea of Marmara, driving southwest down the coast to Fethiye. To buy his boat. He's already found some yachts on the internet, but it is just after the coup attempt in Turkey and many foreign owners have turned their backs on the country. What remains are their yachts, which can now be picked up for a song but aren't always available on the internet. So he visits several marinas. And quickly finds his yacht.

He's interested in a beautiful Maxi 38, which is offered for 60,000 euros. That's his price limit. But there's one problem: Ismail suffers from claustrophobia. The narrowness below deck bothers him. He needs more light and space. So he decides against the Maxi 38 and looks for a deck saloon yacht. Ismail sets a few key factors for his search: the length should be around 40 feet, big enough to be comfortable on the ship, but small enough to be able to handle alone. He finds a Sun Odyssey 40 DS, built in 2001, in excellent condition in Izmir. It's also equipped with a 75 hp engine, a luxury not to be underestimated in the windless months on the south coast. The only problem is: at 80,000 euros the price exceeds Ismail's budget. But like a wink of fate, Ismail gets the biggest order he's ever received at the very same time. In addition, he sells four of his six motorcycles - even though it hurts. But now he has enough money to fulfill his dream of living on the water.

„Wanda" should not only be his new home, but also his companion. First in the Mediterranean, later around the world. His vision is to make „Wanda" a kind of floating backpacker hotel, bringing other people closer to life on the water and with nature.

After he buys the boat in Izmir, he sails first to Datça, remaining in the area for a year. The first thing his friends from the bar give him is the flag of FC Sankt Pauli. Since then, the skull banner is flying from the mast. Every spring he treats his „Wanda" to a new flag from Hamburg, when the old one is ragged. This flag has become his trademark. From Datça, Ismail is drawn to Kaş, where winters are milder and less stormy than in Datça when the wind whistles through the Aegean from the north. In summer, when hardly a breeze stirs in Kaş and it's 40 degrees with the sun blazing in sky, Ismail sails against the wind and cools down.

In spring, when Ismail has just raised the new Pauli flag onto the mast, he sees that his neighbour has also hoisted a German football club flag. Ironically, it's the FC Bayern Munich. The richest club in Germany, which is the total opposite to FC Sankt Pauli. Time for him to set the sail. Wherever the wind will drive him.

More about Ismail and his „Wanda" you will find on
Instagram: @sailingwanda

SUSHI

CLARE ZAC SEX

SAILING

CLARE
36, AUSTRALIA

ZAC
35, ALASKA

Alaskan boy meets Australian girl in Florida. She wants to introduce him to her parents. But the flight is too expensive. Instead, they buy a 40-year-old boat and set sail for Down Under. However an invitation to a wedding in Europe makes them change their plan and conquer the Atlantic. They'll get to Australia one day.

SLOGAN:
„LIVIN A CHAMPAGNE LIFESTYLE ON A LEMONADE WAGE"

START: Florida

STOPP: Mediterranean

DREAM: Australia

HOW IT WORKS?: 3 months work
9 months sailing

BUDGET: 0 $

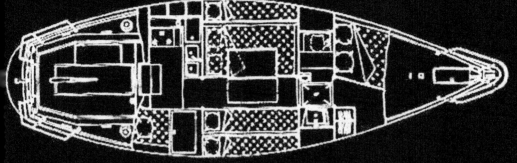

DUFOUR 35
length: 10,74m, beam: 3,45 m, draft: 1,81m

cham pagne

BUILT: 1972
BOUGHT: 2015
PRICE: 15.000 $

The reason for the name of the yacht is obvious. Champagne is Clare's favorite drink, the boat was made in France, three wine racks are installed. And the name can be pronounced anywhere in the world. Cheers!

Zachary doesn't believe his eyes. Who is this person? This blonde angel aboard his friends' catamaran? Zac, as his friends call him, feels like Odysseus meeting the sirens, magically attracted, only he's not tied to the mast. He is alone on board of "Guacamole", an avocado green-painted Irwin 27, a decrepit doer-upper, which has just taken him from the Mississippi Delta to the Florida Keys. Zac's first solo trip lasting several months almost ended in disaster. It wouldn't have taken much and he would have been drowned in the storm somewhere in the Gulf of Mexico, in the middle of the night, among all the oil rigs growing out of the sea like mushrooms in the forest.

His DIY project had started so fantastically. After Zac, a boy from Alaska, had prepared the "Guac," - as he affectionately calls her - for the big trip, he set off to sail from the Florida Keys along the Gulf of Mexico. Past the west coast of Florida, past Alabama and Mississippi. Just in time for the New Year's Eve party on December 31, 2013. Zac, then just 30 years old, arrived in New Orleans / Louisiana. Everything went according to plan. Until the weather turned crazy. It followed an unusually cold January way down below zero degrees. "I couldn't even refuel," says Zac. "All the lines were frozen." So after a few days Zac decided to sail back from the lakes nearby New Orleans to the Florida Keys, where he'd been living on his boat in the marina for several years. There, he repaired boats for their rich owners, took care of maintenance and made a name for himself as an expert in fiberglass work.

Zac opted for the direct route back to Florida. The heat in the Sunshine State attracted him like the compass needle to the North Pole. 550 nautical miles, that had to be done? Zac knew his "Guac" inside out, he trusted her. He had learned to sail on the Irwin 27 when she still belonged to a friend. "Learning by doing" might be Zac's life motto. He never set foot in a sailing school; in general he doesn't have much to do with teachers. He also dropped out of university, never completing his education. Life is his teacher as well as anyone who can teach him something. Through his skill as a craftsman Zac always had enough work to keep afloat. Wherever he was. And that was mostly in marinas in previous years. Make money, invest it in your own boat, go sailing. The triad of his life. Several times he had sailed to the Bahamas with the "Guac". She had become his home, even when he worked on land. Twentyseven feet and almost luxurious, compared to the treehouse he lived in when he came to Miami.

No one expected that Zac would circumnavigate the world in a boat. He is born in Anchorage in 1982. Even though Alaska's largest city is by the sea, there are hardly any sailboats there, and definitely no liveaboards. Often the ocean is covered by a thick layer of ice. In summer, however, his father sometimes takes him to the lakes, where a friend of his has a small catamaran. A hobbie cat. That's how Zac learns to sail. At least a bit. The trips with his father are enjoyable, but they aren't influential, certainly not electrifying.

He moves to Seattle to study, spending two years at university there, but when he has to specialize in a field, he shrugs on his backpack, shuts his dorm door behind him and goes on a walk. Zac has no plan for what to do with his life, so he sets out, hitchhiking through the US for two years, marvelling at the wonderful nature his home-land offers him. Deserts, forests, mountains, lakes - and of course the sea. In order to stay afloat, he works here and there, mostly on construction sites, noting that he has talent in the craft industry. His personal road-trip movie takes him to Oregon where he settles briefly. The reason, of course, is a woman. He buys a pick-up truck, plenty of tools and sets himself up as a carpenter and installer. When the relationship with his girlfriend fails, he climbs behind the wheel of his little truck and drives to Miami, where one of his three sisters lives. This is in 2009. Zac is in his mid-20s.

In Miami he meets Ray. A freaky guy who had formed a kind of hippie community with a few houses. There's a huge garden with tall trees in which small tree houses are built on three floors. Zac is hired as a caretaker and moves into one of the wodden rooms, at the top, just below the crown. The communal garden is as colorful as the inhabitants. He likens it to a zoo. Legend has it that a poor goat wandered the streets of Miami after escaping a bloody voodoo ritual. Ray took care of her. And so she wouldn't be lonely he bought a few other goats. Later Ray expands his private zoo with four emus, several geese, a few turtles, several lizards and even a metre-long python meandering through the green in the middle of Miami's streets.

Ray is not only the owner of several houses, he is also the proud owner of a boat. For Zac this means getting into the yachting scene. Even Ray's boat needs Zac's help. It doesn't take long for Zac to receive commissions from other boat owners. The logical development: He founds his own small marine service business. And so he meets

Matt, the owner of the "Guac", which at that time is still called "Ariel". Zac drives each morning to the ports with his pick-up full of tools; screws, grinds and tinkers on the boats and in the evening he celebrates in the tree house. At the weekend he sails on "Ariel" in the Biscayne Bay. Matt teaches him everything he needs to learn. Sailing, knots, anchors, the whole theory and much more practice.

The following summer, the two sail from Miami to the Bahamas. They start in the late afternoon, sail through the night and reach the archipelago the next day. On this trip Zac succumbs to the fascination of sailing. Shooting stars fall from the sky like snow on a winter's day, the Milky Way shines as bright as a full highway at night. The warm gentle wind drives the small ship over the gigantic ocean to Bimini, a small island, not 50 nautical miles off the coast of the USA where they anchor, dive and fish. They enjoy life on board and parties on the beach. On their way back to Miami, they decide this summer they're going to sail the entire Caribbean. But Matt goes missing the very next day. His car is at the harbour, but "Ariel" is gone. He doesn't even respond to calls. Matt had completely disappeared.

Six months later, Matt reappears out of nowhere. "If life tells you to go, then you have to go," is the only explanation for his disappearance and that has to be good enough. He had sailed back to the Bahamas, working as a mechanic at a diving school, repairing their boats. "Ariel," says Matt, will still be there. He offers Zac a deal. Zac could keep the boat, but he had to return all the tools on board to Matt's father in Connecticut. This is how Zac becomes a boat owner.

"Ariel" is like a messy apartment. It takes days for Zac to rebuild the boat so that he and a friend can sail to Miami with it. But they don't get very far. The outboard motor quits the service, only running for a few minutes, they're up against the wind and the Gulf Stream and they cruise for hours without getting any closer to Florida. And then the US Coast Guard stops by. "Ariel" in her miserable condition is deemed not seaworthy, moreover, she lacks the necessary safety equipment. Zac has to turn back because "Ariel" is not allowed to enter US waters.

In the Bahamas, other yachties help him out. A fire extinguisher here, a signaling device there. On the second attempt, Zac reaches Florida. After his return he leaves his treehouse community and keeps on living on his small sail boat. To save money he anchors in the mangroves. The dinghy, brings him ashore but it has a leak. By happy accident, Zac goes to a Sunday volleyball game in his old community. There he meets a craftsman who runs a small fiberglass workshop in a dodgy suburb. There, they repair and laminate the leaking dinghy. Zac is so adept at dealing with glass fiber reinforced plastics that he is offered work in the workshop. But after two years he lifts the anchor and sails into the Florida Keys. A new world opens up to him.

The sailor community in the Florida Keys is completely different from the one in Miami. In Miami, a yacht is a status symbol and just few owners leave the port. In Marathon on the Keys, Zac meets liveaboards, sailing enthusiasts who cruise the Caribbean or beyond every year after the hurricane season. For $120 a month Zac is allowed to moor on a buoy. He is soon showered with work. His skills, especially in lamination, are fast developing. Spurred on by the sailors and their stories, Zac plans his first major solo tour. He wants to spend three months sailing the US coast along the Gulf of Mexico. His goal: the New Year's Eve party in New Orleans. He puts every dollar he earns into "Ariel", which he refits on the Keys and gives her the distinctive green paint. This is how the little mermaid turns into an avocado. The great adventure of the little Irwin can begin.

However, when he has to flee from the freezing cold after the New Year and sets the shortest course to the Keys, Zac underestimates the unpredictability of the ocean and overestimates his ability to fight fatigue. The Irwin is equipped with a folding keel, perfect for sailing in shallow waters but not for heavy seas. The boat is powered just by a weak outboard motor and the tiller steering is anything but perfect for long one-handed forays over 500 nautical miles. There are neither a chart plotter nor navigational instruments, except for a compass. Zac navigates as he has learned, with maps, his only electronic support being a hand-held GPS, which tells him his current position. He uses it regularly with the chart. But the charts are not up to date. Some oil rigs aren't listed, which spells disaster at night time. Some of the rigs shine like Christmas trees, others are usually redundant and sit unlit like gigantic black spiders on the sea waiting for victims. Zac's plan to sleep half-hourly does not work. The passage demands his full attention. But fatigue is draining him.

When Zac sees the black storm front in the sky one evening, he hopes the storm will sweep over him in half an hour. He is wrong. One of the first gusts tears the foresail, throwing the "Guac" on its side. How strong the wind is, Zac can't say. He also has no anemometer on board. He only notices how the 27 feet under him continue to heel. 30, 40, 50, 60 degrees, and so it goes on and on, until the boat is on the toe rail. Zac climbs higher and higher, then he sits on the side of the hull, which juts vertically into the pitch-black sky. The sharp waves break on the hull, spitting Zac with icy spray. It feels like pebbles. The shreds of the jib beat in the storm, the torn sail is banging on the deck like a sledgehammer. The cold sea looms.

Adrenaline pumps through his body, making him work like a machine. Only when the boat straightens and Zac crawls into the cockpit, does he realise how close he has escaped the sailor's death. He braces the remains of the fore sail, reefs the mainsail to towel size and barricades himself in the cabin. "A boat can do more than its crew," says Zac, leaving himself in "Guac's" safekeeping. "Guac" will take care of him. He tells himself that, he is convinced of that. And so he actually manages some sleep inside, while outside the world around him seems to disappear.

The storm lasts until the next morning. But when Zac crawls back on deck, he is relieved. The storm has subsided, flooding on the "Guac" is limited. Only a few breakers made it into the cabin. He changes course to Tampa Bay. Now with a strong wind aft, he seeks the protection of the coast. He does not want to face another storm. He reaches Tampa Bay in Florida, and has the sails repaired there. Then he continues his journey, back to Marathon on the Keys. He arrives there in mid-February. Exhausted but happy. A little while later he is euphoric.

She stands, on the catamaran belonging to his friends
Hillary and Charles: long blonde hair, a radiant smile.
Like an angel. Or as Zac says, "A fucking hot chick".
Clare! An Australian, a year older than him. Clare is on
a world tour and she's living on his friends' cat for a few
weeks. After a few years of office work in a public agency,
she wanted to see more than files and tables. Like Zac
after graduation, she shouldered her backpack and first
trekked through Central America. In Cuba, she met
Hillary. The two had the same flight, and shared a hotel
room at a stopover. They got along right away. Hillary
invited Clare to the Keys. She could live with them on
the cat. She would find some work in the marina. And
so Clare came to the Keys and scrubbed boats.

The young Australian is an attraction in the marina. An
attractive woman, open-hearted, funny, traveling alone.
A fantasy girl for the lonely hearts on their white yachts.
They all believe they have a chance at landing Clare, but
each one is shipwrecked. However Zac, the craftsman
from Alaska with his 27-foot nutshell, clicks immediately.
"It was his eyes," says Clare. She shrugs. Does she have
any more to say? "The guy is a legend," she adds.

There is only one problem standing in the way of this
young love. And that is: Dad! Zac has promised his
father to go sailing with him for six weeks after his retirement. And that is right now. A totally unimaginable,
threesome on his "Guac". A freshly in love young couple
and in the bunk next door, the old father. "It was like
a cheesy romantic comedy," says Zac. "Ten champagne
corks popped all at once, dolphins jumped out of the sea
and made pirouettes. And then my father is knocking on
the door." But he doesn't want to cancel on his old man,

even if there is no worse time than this, they've had this father-son trip planned for too long.

Friends from the port, Bill and Mara, have the redeeming idea. They take Clare on board and accompany the "Guac". So the two can see each other every now and then, still spend time together. When they are on an island somewhere in the Bahamas, Zac's father gets word that a small plane has just landed on the island. He asks the pilot if he can take him. $50 and a few hours later, father and son say goodbye. Zac's father doesn't want to stand in the way of young love anymore.

Clare and Zac spend three months on the green nutshell, cruising the Caribbean, anchoring in romantic bays, fishing, diving and enjoying togetherness. "It was a great time," says Zac, "with sushi, sex and sailing." Back on the Keys they continue to live on the "Guac".

Shortly thereafter, one of Zac's sisters marries and Clare wants to go to the wedding. "Do you really want to do this to yourself and get to know my whole family?" asks Zac. She wants to. The romance has long since become a relationship. But it's also time for Zac to get to know Clare's parents.

The flight to Australia is expensive. And it's more of a crazy idea than a serious one when Zac asks his girlfriend the absurd question. "Instead of flying, we can buy a bigger boat and sail to Australia," he says. She nods. "Sure, why not." Zac is excited. The "Guac" is definitely too small and too insecure to go around the world on. That's what Zac realized that night in the Gulf of Mexico. The problem is: Both are pretty much cashed out. The new boat should not be expensive.

There is no better place in the US than Miami to buy a yacht. The options are numerous, the prices are low. Quickly, Clare and Zac have put together a list of about ten yachts they want to see. When they enter the third boat on the first day, they know they don't have to search any further. The Dufour 35, built in 1972, is ten years older than the two, but the old lady gives them a feeling of security. It carries the barely pronounceable name "Aotearoa", as the Maoris, the natives of New Zealand, call their homeland. Clare, the Australian, likes that. Zac finds out that the yacht has been there before. So she is seaworthy.

The Dufour belongs to an American Airlines pilot, who lives on it. Not unusual for Miami. Because of the extremely high rents, many people are attracted to the water. Especially those who only visit the city occasionally. The pilot is obviously not a great sailor. The yacht is located on the jetty, connected to the mains. There are no working 12-volt connections nor intact batteries. The anchor windless turns only in one direction, the ropes remind them of aged hippies' dreadlocks. It's even missing a fridge. The pilot preferred to dine in restaurants. Nevertheless, the two make an offer. The best argument for buying is the price: $15,000. Exactly one year after Clare and Zac met, they are the proud owners of a Dufour. They immediately decide to change the name. With every radio contact, in every port there are the same questions: "What is the name of the ship? How is that written?" But there's nothing going to stand in the way of the Australian adventure.

They transfer the boat to the Florida Keys. For almost two years, the two work on the ship and they baptize her "Champagne". An apt name choice. Champagne is Clare's favorite drink, the boat is French and even if it is poorly equipped, it does have wine racks. In addition, "Bubbly" pretty much describes their disposition. Clare and Zac are in a champagne mood.

At the end of July 2015, the refit of "Champagne" is in full swing, Zac wants to ask his Clare, whom he calls SeaJay, the question of all questions. In the early morning he leaves the ship, allegedly to drive to a job. Instead, he drives to the beach. The tide has washed up a wide swath of algae and seaweed. It smells of the sea and decaying fish. Meter by meter Zac pulls the flotsam vegetation on the beach to form two and a half meter tall words: "SeaJay, marry me!?" It takes six hours. The lettering occupies half the beach. Then he calls Clare. Zac has long hired a pilot to fly them over the beach so Clare can read his proposal. He's thought of everything, even the fishing line. The machine is an old rickety biplane. The pilot, who is in on Zac's plan, advises him to tie the engagement ring to his pants with a string. If it falls down inside the draughty machine, it'll disappear into the bowels of the flying monster never to be seen again.

When Clare picks up the phone, she feels uncomfortable. She's a little bit mad that Zac wants to pick her up now to show her something, it doesn't float her boat. She would much rather rest. But in the end, she agrees. It seems important to him.

First she is surprised that Zac gives her a flight over the Florida Keys. Then she is surprised by the marriage proposal. And then that Zac ends the question with an exclamation mark and then sets a question mark. The machine roars so loud that conversation is impossible. Both wear earmuffs, but without microphones. Zac looks at Clare, gives a thumbs up, then tilts is thumb down. Zac shrugs his shoulders questioningly. Then Clare raises her fist and the thumb points upwards. The two are engaged.

They celebrate the wedding a year later. In September, somewhere in the middle of nowhere in Oregon. A small ceremony, only the families arrive from Alaska and Australia. They all live together in a hut in the woods, have a barbecue by the campfire, enjoying the simple life. Clare bought a tight white dress for $12. Her wedding dress. Even though the families know each other now, that doesn't change the plan to sail to Australia. In November 2016, Clare and Zac set sail. "Champagne" is ready to conquer the world.

The trail first takes them to the Bahamas, where their romance began. From there they want to sail across the Caribbean towards Venezuela, then through the Panama Canal into the Pacific. That is the plan. But they only get to Puerto Rico. When Zac's sister and her husband come aboard for a few days, they catch a wonderfully big fish. The next day they are all sick, have chills and fever at the same time. They feel weak and miserable. The only toilet on board becomes a hotly contested favorite place. At first, they believe in a normal food poisoning that passes quickly, but then a doctor diagnoses a very different problem. The fish had become infected with an aggressive type of bacteria that only exists on special reefs.

Ciguatera is the name of the special kind of fish poisoning. The infection takes place via the consumption of fish, in whose body the Ciguatoxin enriched itself.

The treacherous truth: The poison is not destroyed by cooking and affects neither the appearance nor the taste of the fish. A typical sign of Ciguatera is the reversal of the warm-cold sensation. Contact with cold air or cold drinks is perceived as hot. Even if the gastrointestinal symptoms disappear after a few days, the nerve disorders can last for months. The four only recover slowly. In addition, there is another problem: "Champagne" has rudder damage and must be lifted out of the water, so Zac, as soon as he is feeling better, can repair it. Valuable time passes.

In the meantime, April is turning into May and the winds are favorable to cross the Atlantic from the Caribbean. In addition, in just a few weeks, three friend couples celebrate their weddings in Europe. Once again, both decide to save on the cost of the plane.

The ARC is in the starting point, a transatlantic regatta for cruising sailors. But when they see the entry fee prices and the demands made on the yachts, they decide against official participation, but they do decide to travel around the 200+ yachts, so they at least don't feel all alone on the wide ocean.

From Puerto Rico, Clare and Zac sail 900 nautical miles to Bermuda. About 100 nautical miles per day. As they pass the infamous Bermuda Triangle, their brand new chart plotter actually drops out. For Zac, who is used to navigating maps, that's not a problem, but they'll have to make another unplanned stop and ship the device to Florida for repair. It takes three weeks to return. From the Bermudas they then sail to the Azores, a passage of about 1700 miles. After 17 partly stormy, but mostly boring days on board with changing strata they reach the Portuguese archipelago. Whales accompany them on the last few nautical miles, the green mountains rise majestically from the water. The two would have liked to stay there longer, but they have appointments - the three weddings. From the Azores it is another 1000 nautical miles to Gibraltar. In July 2017 they reach the European mainland. They conquered the Atlantic on their 45-year-old yacht. They celebrate - of course with champagne.

Back from the wedding triathlon, they set sail again. They celebrate wild parties in Ibiza, hiking in Mallorca, visit Barcelona and land in Sardinia. However, because they are only allowed to stay in the EU for a maximum of three months, they have to leave European waters. They head south. Tunisia is their destination. "Champagne" is supposed to overwinter in Monastir. Zac flies back to Florida to make money, Clare does the same in Australia.

In the spring they continue their tour. From Tunisia they now head north. They circle Sicily, sail to the Aeolian Islands, admire the volcanic island of Stromboli. To save money, they don't dock, but anchor in wild coves, shop at the market and go to restaurants only once a week. "Sometimes our lives are reminiscent of retirees," says Zac, laughing. "We go to bed early, read books or watch a movie".

From Italy, it's time for another few days in Albania, again, the ship must leave the EU. From there, "Champagne" travels through the Greek islands, sailing in the ancient footsteps of Odysseus. For winter they choose Kaş in Turkey, again a place outside the EU. The engine has to be overhauled, it rattles and leaks oil. Clare and Zac don't stay in Turkey all winter. They leave to make money again. Just as every other winter. The triad of their life. Working, investing in the yacht, sailing. "Luckily we have a small boat," says Zac. He knows the bill only too well: small ships, small money. Big ships, big money.

They haven't lost sight of their goal: Australia. They have rejected the idea of sailing through the Suez Canal into the Red Sea and then through the Indian Ocean, even if it is the shortest route. For one, the route is dangerous because of the pirates and secondly, the wind would be against them. "We sail back through the Mediterranean," says Zac. Then across the Canaries and Cape Verde back across the Atlantic. To South America and then through the Panama Canal, as they had planned, before they spontaneously came to Europe. At least that's the plan. But what are plans?

Her tour around the world is a bit reminiscent of Forrest Gump. "Sailing is like a box of chocolates - you never know where to go next".

You want to follow the trip of Clare and Zac? Have a look at www.bottlehalffull.org

MR. SUNSHINE

MARK

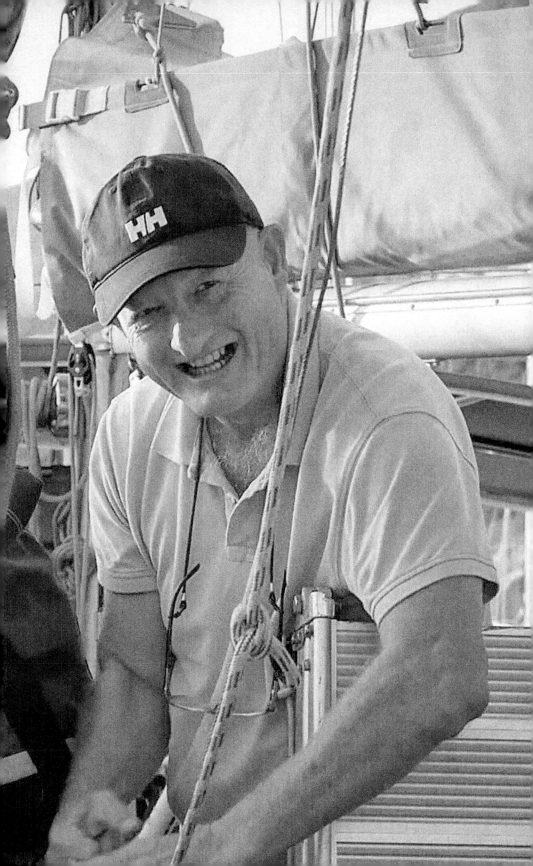

zinga

Mark's father named the yacht. In an African language, 'Zinga' supposedly means 'King of the Seas'. Only later Mark discoverd the same name on an Indian menu: in Hindu stands for 'Scampi'.

BUILT: 1982
PRICE: INHERITED
VALUE: PRICELESS

MAURITIUS 43, BY BRUCE ROBERTS
lenght: 13,18 m, beam: 3,96m, draft: 1,80m

MARK

60, SOUTH AFRICA

PROFIT: Enjoying life

LOSS: 25 kilograms

PROFESSION: Entrepreneur

ONCE UPON A TIME: Hare Krishna

After the death of his father, Mark leaves South Africa to live in the Mediterranean Sea on board his deceased father's yacht. At sea he finds what he has been seeking for so long, peace and tranquility, something he could not even find in Tibetan monasteries. The Turks call him ‚gülen amca", the smiling uncle.

When the first rays of winter sun kiss the ‚sleeping giant' above the town of Kaş and disperse the gray of the night, the trees on the mountains take form and the gentle waves of the Mediterranean Sea glitter and sparkle. This is also the hour that Mark begins his day. As always, it's going to be a fantastic day.

In June 2017 Mark, the South African, sailed his ketch to the small Greek island of Kastellorizo and anchored in front of the panorama of churches, the old fortress and the restaurants on the hillside, all painted bright blue with whitewashed walls, the colors of the sky.

Lowering his dinghy into the water, he went ashore and found himself in a dreamlike location where just 492 people call home. Mark dined in one of the typical Greek tavernas and got talking to Alexander and Gayle. They lived on board their yacht ‚Stefana' just 3 nautical miles away in the new marina in Kaş, Turkey.

A day later Mark sailed around the peninsula of Kaş, which protrudes like a finger into the sea, parallel to the Turkish coast and found himself in a beautiful bay protected from wind and waves. He sailed past the shallow slopes with the pretty mansions and when he reached the head of the bay, just past the marina pontoons, he dropped the anchor of his yacht along with the anchor of his life. He had arrived. He sensed that all of his life's ups and downs had led him to this place and this point in time.

Mark was captivated by the bustling town of Kaş with its many restaurants and bars, the charming little streets, the old-fashioned atmosphere, the pleasant tourism, a mix of young divers from major Turkish cities and older people from all over the world who had chosen Kaş as their adopted home.

The hour-long journey from the nearest airport via twisting roads that wind through the mountains keep the package tourists far away. The people who come to Kaş, this small harbour town by the sea, are looking for peace and relaxation - on land, on the water, but mostly under water.

On the day of his arrival Mark signs a mooring contract for three years at the marina. A decision he has never regretted.

Every morning, when Mark rouses from the belly of his ‚Zinga‘ he does his stretch exercises up in the cockpit, squints into the sun, which is still low over the mountains in the east, and then takes a deep breath, as if soaking in the energy of the sun‘s rays so they can put a smile on his face for the rest of the day.

For a long moment the 60-year-old remains motionless with his eyes closed. Then he turns to his neighbor on the yacht next door, touches his beige baseball cap, pulls the cap off his completely bald head and bows politely. A new day begins with the same words: „Good morning! What a beautiful day!“ Then he laughs his distinctive laugh, loud and rough. The day‘s fun has begun and Mark carries the smile on his face like a trademark. „Oh man, you look like crap this morning“. His neighbor listens to the jovial banter before being invited over for a coffee. „I think you could use one,“ says Mark, quickly disappearing below deck and almost as quickly reappearing on deck with a thermos of freshly brewed awake-maker. Mark drinks his coffee black, but always has milk on board for his guests. „Do you want some French toast? I can do that. I just have to go get eggs. No problem!" He waddles along the pontoon in his sandals, greets here, laughs there. If you want to know where Mark is, you just have to listen. Eventually you'll hear the laughter coming from somewhere.

Mark collects phone numbers and contacts like children collect football cards of the World Cup, he knows everyone in the marina. Not just the sailors. He also calls every employee of the marina by name, chats with them as best he can, listens. He taps the man at the cash register in the supermarket heartily, he asks a craftsman, how his daughter is doing, she was recently ill. And while the man answers Mark waves to the chattering scooter roaring along the marina quay and shouts, „Merhaba! Nasılsın?" Hello, how are you? The man on the scooter beams and laughs: „Maaaaaaark!" He raises his thumb, nods and stops briefly to shake hands with the usual reply. „Iyi" Mark replies and laughs loudly, „çok iyi". Very good.

Of course, Mark is excellent. Nobody would expect it to be any different. Mark is Mr. Sunshine. The Turks in the marina call him ‚gülen amca', the uncle with the smile.

They respect how hard he tries to speak their language in his open-hearted way. He did eagerly begin Turkish language lessons, but after a few times he gave it up. „Too much homework." says Mark laughing. There's simply no time for that.

Everyone in the marina knows the man from the southern tip of Africa. Everyone likes him. It's not possible to dislike him. His laughter is contagious, his good mood unique and he has his own dance style. When musicians play in the marina bar in the evening, Mark jumps up off his seat, shrugs his shoulders, snaps his fingers and claps along.

Mark is always ready to listen too. Always there to lend a helping hand. Mark is the glue that holds the community of sailors together. „May I introduce you to..." is one of his well-known opening lines, which is typical for him. He loves to bring people together. He organizes cooking classes, invites you to eat, sets up the barbecue. If someone has a problem Mark generally has the right solution.

When the girlfriend of a friend badly breaks her ankle, Mark drives her to the hospital, clarifies the formalities with the doctors and stays the night at the hospital. After surgery, he takes her to the airport, waiting patiently until she is safely on the plane. Mark has many things of his own to attend to. His aging yacht urgently needs a refit and he's looking to buy an apartment in Kas. But all this can wait, if a friend is in need. Even though he met her only a few days ago.

Some days he seems over-excited and restless, as if he doesn't know what to do with all of his energy. He rushes from one appointment to the next: yoga, language class, lunch, coffee, beer, or wine at the bar. And then he's rushing off on his scooter to meet someone for a dinner date.

Mark loves the new life he's living in Turkey on board his yacht ‚Zinga'. It's a far cry from his life in South Africa where for a long time he did not receive any recognition from his family. „Actually, I was always the outsider in a group." Mark says in a quiet moment of reflection.

Mark was born in June 1959 in Salisbury, today's Harare, the capital of Zimbabwe. The first 13 weeks of his life are spent in an incubator, his twin brother only survives for five days. His parents, both from England, leave Rhodesia when Mark is three years old, his younger brother Brett is barely one year old. The young family move to South Africa and settle in Johannesburg. John, his father, starts a company that specializes in retreading tires. In the coming decades, his father forges ahead so that the small company becomes the market leader in South Africa. The company produces tire treads, supplies the raw material to customers, and provides technical service. Today, 50 years later, the company employs over 300 people. Since the end of 2018, the Italian tread manufacturer Marangoni holds a majority stake of 51 percent in the family business. Mark's younger brother Brett is the managing director and continues to run the business successfully and its growing from strength to strength. A position which had once been Mark's, a long long time ago.

During his school days Mark is an avid dinghy sailor. He buys a 16 Hobie cat, then an 18 Hobie cat and sails as much as he can. He inherited the passion for the sea from his father. In the early 80s his father buys the shell of a Mauritius 43 , designed by Bruce Roberts as a true blue water yacht from a yacht builder called VHV Marine in Honeydew South Africa. The plan is to fit her out in South Africa to suit their personal requirements. Mark assisted his father in managing the two-year fitting of the ketch, a two masted yacht.

While Zinga is being finished off, Mark works in an accounting firm and studies economics at the University of South Africa (Unisa). His father names the yacht ‚Zinga‘, which means ‚king of the sea‘ in an African language. It was not until many years later, during a visit to India, that Mark discovers a restaurant with ‚Tandoori Zinga‘ on the menu. Scampi, cooked in the traditional Indian tandoori oven.

In Durban harbor in December 1983 Mark cracks a bottle of champagne on the hull of the yacht ‚Zinga‘ and the vessel becomes the ‚king of the sea‘ for him and his father and the family. For two more months Mark lives on board and oversees the Israeli carpenter‘s finishing touches which gives the yacht an elegant, maritime look. Sadly, the maiden voyage ends in disaster after less than a mile. Mark and his father have mounted the exhaust manifold the wrong way around which leads to engine failure as water is sucked into the engine. As soon as ‚Zinga‘ is back at the marina the engine is thoroughly flushed and the manifold is refitted correctly.

Apart from giving sailing pleasure, ‚Zinga‘ has a secondary potential purpose in case the family needs to leave South Africa. As was the case in Rhodesia, Mark‘s father distrusts the political stability in his new homeland. The plan is to head for Greece if things fall apart. He‘s read a lot about Greece even if he‘s never been there. Things don‘t fall apart but the plan still matures to bring ‚Zinga‘ to Rhodes. By sea, but not under her own sail. ‚Zinga‘

takes a piggy-back ride on a freighter which brings her to Trieste, Italy.

Mark is entrusted with taking ‚Zinga‘ on the passage from Trieste along the Italian coast to Rhodes. From time to time his father comes on board to monitor his eldest son‘s progress and enjoy the dream of sailing, visiting new places and meeting new people. Making his work efforts even more rewarding.

Immediately after leaving Trieste, the five-member crew find themselves in good company. It seems that several yachts are taking the same route to Venice. The crew eagerly set out to push ‚Zinga‘ hard as if they were sailing in a regatta. It‘s only once they arrive in Venice well ahead of the rest of the yachts that they realize they have actually been mixed up in a real rally regatta, without officially participating in it.

From there Mark begins a wonderful three months sailing his father‘s yacht to Rhodes, . Along the Italian coast, always heading south. Then the Adriatic melts into the Aegean Sea and they sail through a world of Greek islands. They visit Turkey and finally deliver the boat to Rhodes. Mark flies back to South Africa, ‚Zinga‘ stays in Greece and his father buys a house on the small island of Symi. Every year, Mark then spends several weeks sailing the Mediterranean Sea with friends.

Back in South Africa Mark goes to work for his father‘s company. But there‘s no special treatment, even though he is the son of the owner, Mark has to work his way up. He learns the business from scratch, works for 30 years in sales, maintains customer contacts, builds branches until he becomes managing director of the company, alongside his younger brother Brett.

Bret had a technical training to learn the trade ‚The German Continental in Port Elizabeth hires him, as does the American Oliver Rubber Company in San Francisco. Eventually he returns to Johannesburg to modernize and run the production line of their family business.

In 1987, Mark is sent to London. The idea is to promote expansion of the business into Europe, Scandinavia and the Middle East. During this time, he meets Clare, a young South African woman. He falls in love with her. The two marry, but the marriage lasts only five years.

In 1992, his father orders his firstborn back to South Africa. This is the beginning of a fracture in the father-son relationship. When Mark visits his father in Greece at his summer residence and wants to go sailing with ‚Zinga, as he had in previous summers, his father forbids him to leave the harbor. Mark is allowed to live on board ‚Zinga‘, but is not allowed to untie the lines. This lack of trust begins to eat at Mark‘s soul.

As time passes Mark becomes more and more unhappy, eats food to comfort his feelings and gains weight until he reaches 125 kilos (275 pounds). Mark finds other business interests in South Africa. He partners up in two Italian restaurants. One even bearing his name. To give it a more authentic Italian feel he calls it ‚Marcos‘. The other ‚Tito‘s‘. Mark laughs. „At that time, I was my best customer!“

When Mark reaches his 50th birthday he decides to leave the family business. The tensions within the family have pushed him to this point. The separation leaves Mark with an income, but he suffers personally from the situation. He becomes an entrepreneur, founding a recycling company for rubber products in South Africa. He is proud of what he has built, but neither his father nor his brother ever visits his new company. The expected backing and recognition he sought never manifests. Things fall apart, there is no success story.

The once happy Mark is becoming more and more serious, dissatisfied, grumpier. Mark's father and his second wife believe that he is bipolar because of his mood swings. „You have mental health problems" they say to him. But a doctor simply states that Mark has diabetes brought on by being overweight. The changes in mood are due to hypoglycemia.

At this time, while professionally and privately isolated, Mark accepts the offer to conquer the Atlantic. With seven people on board, he assists in a transfer of an 80-foot catamaran from Cape Town to Brazil. But already at the Cape of Good Hope they get into a storm that damages the cat. They have to turn around and repair the ship, then set off again for the second time. The trail leads them to Saint Helena, a small island in the middle of the South Atlantic. And then, because his fellow sailors run out of cigarettes, they decide to make a detour of 700 nautical miles to replenish their stocks on Ascension Island. As a ship's cook Mark ruins his reputation just a few days into the trip when he boils the pasta in sea water. „Salt water is salt water", Mark had thought. A fallacy. The Atlantic has ruined the pasta. Of course, Mark laughs as he retells the story.

Back from the transatlantic passage there is work waiting for him in the family business. One last chance. His 30 years of sales experience are needed in India. So, he gets on a plane, negotiates and loses the deal. Disappointed and dismayed Mark loses himself in India. During this time, he gets to know Tibetan monks, wanders from monastery to monastery and finally finds himself in the arms of the Hindu sect Hare Krishna. He meditates, bathes in the Ganges, nourishes himself with vegetarian food and wears the white robe of the disciple.

He reads the scriptures of Buddhism and Hinduism, the Sutras, Gita and the Vinaya, once, twice. Five times. They give him a lot. But they don't give him everything he's looking for. „Life is one neverending experience." says Mark. And so, his journey to his Hare Krishna existence is just one chapter of many in his life.

Back in South Africa he again dedicates himself to his own projects. He is working with partners to finance the construction of a residential complex for black students. Another project is the treatment of wastewater. „I need the mental activity." he says. Even though he could, he doesn't want to retire yet.

When his father dies in 2017, he sits down with his brother and talks about the family heritage. They both agree that Mark will not be going back to the family business. He and his brother's views on life and business are too different. But even outside the business he gets his financial share of the company, which is now a public limited company and a joint venture with the Italians of Marangoni. „Why" asks his brother, „don't you go and live on Zinga and live the dream?" The once proud yacht has grown old and tired looking and has received little care. A comprehensive refit is the way forward.

Mark likes the idea of bringing ‚Zinga' back to her former glory. He remembers the summers he spent on the yacht with friends. The transfer trip from Trieste to Rhodes. The silent and the beautiful moments. And because he was probably happier nowhere else than on board ‚Zinga' that linked him so much with his father. He had also felt the peace he found meditating in India when sailing on the open sea. So once again he turns his back on South Africa to open the next chapter of his life.

The simple life on board ‚Zinga' does Mark good. He loses over 25 kilos (55 pounds), his blood sugar levels are the best they've been in years. But most of all his laughter has returned. He is feeling fit and well all around. His joie de vivre is back, which he has missed for so long.

Every day he steps out into the cockpit of ‚Zinga' and says „Good morning! What a beautiful day!" Then he laughs his distinctive laugh, loud and rough. It's good to be alive.

Mark's life lessons learned to date:

Forgive easily.
Be Mindful of your thoughts and actions.
Live today in the present as yesterday is gone and tomorrow has not materialised.
Always avail yourself to serve others.
Keep smiling be calm, breathe and approach all from a position of Love.

There is a saying:

If you want to make God laugh, tell him your plans !!!

Nameste

Mr. Sunshine is pretty new on Instagram. Check his account: @msprosontr

JIM
ON THE
RUN

acher

Acheron was the British Navy submarine on which Jim's father was an officer. The name is a tribute to his father, who died when Jim was young.

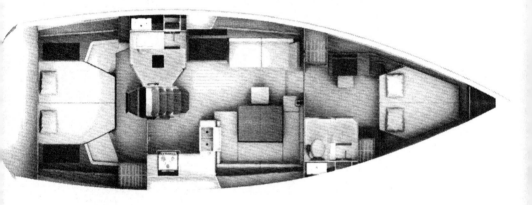

SUN ODYSSEY 44 DS
length: 13,34m, beam: 4,24 m, draft: 2,2 m

BUILT: 2018
BOUGHT: 2018
PRICE: 280.000 €

on

JIM

63, ENGLAND

PROFESSION: Entrepreneur

PASSION: nude art photography

HATES: CFS-Syndrom

LIKES: Gin & Tonic

Jim is a passionate nude art photographer. He sees his art as a tribute to God, whom he believes he encountered at a young age. After many personal and professional ups and downs in his life, his small business thrives in Scotland. But suddenly he thinks he has violated US export rules. In a touch of paranoia he already sees himself in a US jail. That's why he's preparing his escape. He wants to flee in a sail boat and settle in the Cape Verde Islands. But he has to learn to sail first.

Andorra? What does he know about Andorra? 80,000 inhabitants, a principality in the Pyrenees, sandwiched between France and Spain, with a handful of banks and three ski resorts. Could he live here? If his worst fears were true, if his doubts were justified, then it would be a journey of no return. Jim does not have to think twice. A strangling grip tightens his throat as he imagines himself in Andorra. No, he doesn't see himself in Andorra.

What about Cape Verde? This African archipelago in the Atlantic off the coast of Senegal has no extradition agreement with the US authorities. Jim has gleaned this from online research one night as once again sleep eludes him. He visualizes himself escaping there. Yes, he can imagine himself retiring to Cape Verde.

But how would this Brit, who set up his small business in Scotland, get there? Jim's brain methodically works through all the possible ways to get from Scotland to Cape Verde. He's been physically suffering for years. He has some good times, but also a lot of bad ones. Now though, his health is declining.

Could he go by plane? No, he'd be refused entry! He imagines that he'd be arrested at the gate, dragged away in handcuffs like a felon. But he is just a harmless businessman from Dundee. His company, which specializes in monitoring systems, sells high-tech equipment for oil companies and power plants all over the world. Also in the US and in countries that are not necessarily considered America's best allies.

Had Jim not accidentally read an article about a British entrepreneur who was extradited to the US for violating US export rules and was facing a potential sentence of 30 years imprisonment, he probably wouldn't have fallen into this paranoia which is almost driving him crazy.

So Cape Verde! It seems the only way to get there unmolested and anonymous is by sea. All he has to do is take a boat from Scotland until he's almost at the equator. Almost at the equator? Jim quickly realizes that no motorboat has fuel tanks anywhere near large enough to handle this gigantic passage of nearly 3,000 nautical miles nonstop. And at every refueling stop, he would run the risk of falling into the hands of his captors. In Jim's logic, there is only one option: he has to learn to sail.

So he enrolls at a sailing school on the west coast of Scotland to become a skipper. Nobody else is privy to his plans. He doesn't share his worries with anyone. If he had done, he would have quickly realized that his panic is unfounded. But then he would never have learned to sail - and would not be living on his own yacht 'Acheron' in the Mediterranean today, planning a circumnavigation of the world.

He doesn't even tell his wife his real motive. «What do you think about learning to sail together, darling,» he asks her, as innocuously as possible. She finds the idea appealing. That was in the summer of 2012. And Jim was in his 50s.

Jim is 63 years old today. An unobtrusive and reserved man in a polo shirt with a neatly trimmed beard, which the years have colored white. He speaks with a gently cultured English accent and every evening sees him enjoying his ritual gin and tonic. You could say Jim is 'very British'.

He compares sailing with a spiritual experience. «At sea I can breathe freely,» he says. And he doesn't mean that only in a metaphorical sense. Jim is struggling with respiratory problems. But when he leaves the land behind, his problems get smaller and smaller, the ocean gets bigger and bigger. When he's alone on the sea, an inconspicuous sail in this vast expanse, Jim truly feels free. Altruistic by nature, he wants to share this experience. Jim's vision is to invite as many people as possible from different countries and cultures to his 'Acheron' to experience this indescribable sense of freedom.

To accurately understand why it is so special that Jim can lead a happy life on his sailing yacht today, you have to go back to his childhood.

Jim's love of the sea was born in the cradle. It's nurtured on the south coast of England, in Weymouth in the county of Dorset, a popular resort, known for its miles of sandy beaches. His father serves in the Royal Navy as a chief petty officer on a submarine called 'Acheron'. Whenever 'Acheron' returns to base after three months at sea, then little Jim is often taken on board. The submarine is his adventure playground. Everyone on the crew knows little Jim. And everyone likes the shy boy. «Those were happy moments,» he remembers. Happy instants in an otherwise rather unhappy childhood. He often reminisces about that time, on quiet evenings when he sits in the cockpit of his yacht, which he named after the submarine on which his father served. His father died tragically when Jim was just 25 years old.

Jim's life was never easy. His childhood ends abruptly when, aged 15, he joined the Royal Air Force. There he becomes a technician with expertise in aircraft navigation systems. His first post takes him to the far north of Scotland. He lives in the barracks with 3000 men and a handful of women, sharing four man rooms. «It was like a monastery,» says Jim. «A monastery in which all conversations were only about football, sex and airplanes."

In the military world dominated by chauvinism and machismo, the sensitive boy from the South of England feels like an alien. His comrades' focus is totally on sex, they don't know any other topic. Walls and locker doors are covered with cheap pin-up photos. He feels uncomfortable in the barracks. He loves classical music, reads profusely and philosophizes about the universe. He's sure there must be more. Something deeper. So unlike his Air Force associates, Jim has a different focus. He doesn't look for cheap thrills and fast sex, but for something more meaningful. He's searching for the purpose of life - and to find God.

Jim is not religious though. He gets nothing out of Sunday church visits, when all the airmen put on their blue dress uniform and march to church. But then he reads the Bible and in particular the Gospel of John. This impresses him. And overnight he decides to become a Christian. So he prays to God and tells him that from now on he will believe in Jesus and follow Him.

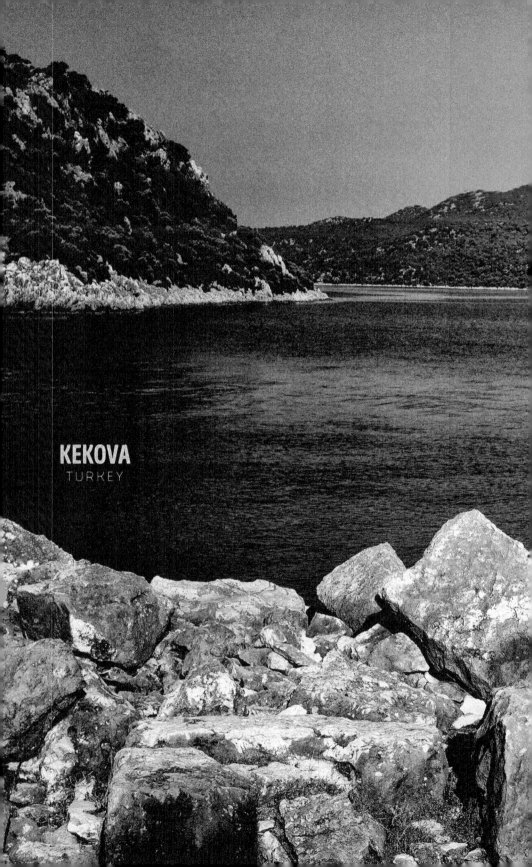

KEKOVA
TURKEY

Jim expects some confirmation, an obvious sign of acknowledgement, but nothing happens. So he prays again the next day, and the next, but still nothing happens. That's how it works for three months. A quarter of a year after his decision, while his roommates are sleeping, he kneels down next to his bed, puts his hands together and calls to God: «I cannot live another day without knowing you. Please reveal yourself to me». After that he crawls back into bed, relieved that none of his room mates have seen him praying.

The next day Jim is sitting in his room, listening to some music, Handel's «Messiah». He only dares listen to classical music when he's alone. It is then that, what Jim calls his 'spiritual experience', happens. The room was suddenly filled with an indescribable presence. First he just sits there, frozen in awe. «I knew there was someone else there.» Then the presence surrounds him, breaks like a wave over him. «It was wonderful. It is impossible to adequately describe what that presence conveyed. Love, certainly, but also perfection and wholeness. The completion of all things and the answer to every question you have ever had. I felt protected. And safe,» says Jim.

Jim is 17 years old at the time of this experience. He's sitting in this dreary room in these lackluster barracks in the north of Scotland, with walls full of pornographic rubbish. At this moment, he promises God to honor His creatures and portray them in all their beauty. At that moment, he decides to become a nude art photographer. He smiles mischievously. «I know,» he grins. «That sounds completely confused. But that's how it was.» But it will still be 20 years before Jim composes his first nude art photo.

At the age of 21 Jim marries. The marriage soon descends into what feels like martyrdom, leaving deep scars. This too, is not to be understood merely in a figurative sense. Jim doesn't like to talk about that time. Certainly not about the woman he once loved. She is much older than him and brings two children into the marriage. Then she becomes pregnant again, to Jim, giving birth to two girls. Twins. Jim is proud of his daughters. One is a helicopter pilot in the Air Force and flew missions in Afghanistan; the other moved to Australia and works as a wedding stylist.

But Jim doesn't find happiness in his marriage. At first his wife dominates him, then she bullies him. Trying to keep up with his wife's demands, they live beyond their means, at one point even owning twelve horses. At the age of 25 Jim leaves the Royal Air Force. His income is nowhere near enough to fulfill his wife's wishes. He tries working as a rep. First for vacuum cleaners, then for copiers, later for technical equipment used by oil companies. With each new job, the family moves home, crisscrossing Scotland.

Jim works from dawn well into the night, but the money is never enough. At home he feels like a prisoner. Around this time he begins sailing a small dinghy for the first time on Loch Ore. Sailing lets him enjoy a few hours of freedom. As an escape from his wife. What initially connected him to her has become a burden. "She only played classical music in the house. A whole decade of music history has passed me by,» says Jim. «Abba, for example, was not allowed to be heard in our house.»

Jim goes independent, selling goods on commission. But he's accumulating more and more debt. By 1986 he is broke. Insolvent. He can't pay any more bills. Cheques bounce, the electricity is turned off and the landlord evicts the family. Once again they have to move. Because the mail doesn't reach them, an enforcement order can't be served and the authorities are now looking for him. When the police find him, he's arrested and taken away in handcuffs. It's the most shameful moment in Jim's life. Even if he is released after only one night in a cell.

Jim realizes that he needs to save himself and to do that he has to separate from his wife. At the age of 37 he leaves his wife and children and moves temporarily to a friend's house in Dundee. When asked about it today, he says, «My first marriage was hell.»

After the break, Jim's life seems to begin working out for the better. He finds a new job, his own apartment and meets Rosie, who becomes his second wife. After nine months they move in together. Shortly afterwards, Rosy becomes pregnant. Jim, who's already raised four children, feels overwhelmed. He is always tired, his muscles hurt, he is run down and he has sleep apnoea. He also suffers from high blood pressure and occasional anxiety. The odyssey from doctor to doctor is torture for him. He has the impression that nobody is taking his suffering seriously, nor can diagnose any specific disease. It takes a long time until he finds a doctor who diagnoses chronic fatigue syndrome (CFS). CFS is a disease that had hardly been researched until recently. One symptom is persistent exhaustion. «It feels like a fever,» says Jim. "Only without a temperature".

Jim is unable to work, so he quits his job. He is self-employed again, selling commission-based supplies for oil companies and power plants. His bed is his office. So from here he makes phone calls. Then he sleeps a little bit. And when he wakes up, he orders stock. He's had to sell his car, so he drives to his customers by motorbike from Edinburgh where he lives now, to Aberdeen. 120 miles, in the rain, sleet and cold. Despite his physical limitations. He stows his motorcycle gear in the saddlebags, then meets the customer. «I felt shitty,» says Jim. Nevertheless, he's been able to keep himself and his family afloat for two years. Then he changes the business and builds a company as a technical components supplier.

In 1998, Jim has an idea that should catapult his business forward. He is the first company in this highly specialized segment to create a website. In times of fax machines and analog modems, this is a real revolution. Because he can't afford a programmer, Jim designs his own website. «That was a really horrible website,» says Jim, laughing. «It was very simple. But it contained all the information about the products, plus the price. And on every page was my phone number and address.»

Taking advantage of the internet, this small Scottish one-man business suddenly reaches customers worldwide, defying the competition from huge businesses such as Siemens and Honeywell. It doesn't take long for Jim to have 15 employees. The business is thriving. Again and again, chronic fatigue symptoms force him to his knees, but he always manages to get back up. And then, in 2012, he suddenly panics when he reads the article about the British businessman who was extradited to the Unit-

ed States. But instead of checking to see if his company really violated US export rules, Jim forges ahead with his escape plan to Cape Verde.

He trains as a skipper in Scotland and Gibraltar. The following spring, he charters a Bavaria 38 in Flensburg, sailing with his family through the Danish South Seas. He is feeling well. And free. For the first time in a long time. Just like when he allowed himself a few hours of freedom from his first wife on Loch Ore. «I felt that the sea has the power to recalibrate my soul,» says Jim.

In autumn he charters a boat in Scotland. It is bitterly cold, but Jim enjoys the days at sea. After the trip he wants to buy his own boat. Not as a hobby, but as a cure. It doesn't have to be that big, let alone bring him to Cape Verde, because Jim's now discovered that he didn't break any US laws after all.

Jim buys a used Beneteau First 35. He sails with friends, first on the coasts of Scotland, then on to Denmark. He retreats further from his business, learning to rely on his managers and employees and to be able to make important decisions from a distance. Weekly Skype conferences are enough to run this good team with expertise and confidence.

Initially, Jim reluctantly sails alone. But because of his exhaustion, he doesn't dare to sail far, as time and again, draining fatigue attacks him abruptly and without warning. But the longer he is at sea, the better he becomes, so he spends longer and longer periods sailing his yacht single-handed.

One day he finds himself alone on board, steering straight into a storm in the Kattegat. Alone at the tiller, without an autopilot. The wind violently shakes the shrouds, throwing the boat from side to side. Waves pile up meters high. As always, Jim listens to music for reassurance. He has hundreds of songs stored on his iPhone and can play them in random order on the cockpit speakers. Suddenly Jim is devoured by a wall of thick fog. He feels like he's in cotton wool, like a plane going through the clouds. Flying blind. Visibility drops below 50 meters. At this very moment, his iPhone plays Mozart's Requiem. Funeral music.

Two thoughts flash through Jim's mind. The first: «Shit, I'm going to die.» The second: «Steve Jobs is having a laugh at my expense.» And then, like the Flying Dutchman, a ship hurtles out of the fog at him and rushes past. He misses a collision by only 20 meters on that stormy Baltic Sea. But Jim knows that if he gives up, the yacht will sink. And so he defies the rough sea, celebrating every wave that washes over his boat. He feels alive. He jettisons the fear. «I felt like in the movie, The Boat,» Jim laughs.

During this trip through Denmark, he also sails to Kolding port and visits Nordship shipyard. He falls in love with a used Nordship 35 and buys it without a second thought. The following year he sails it through the Kiel Canal to Cuxhaven, from there via Helgoland to Scotland, a total of 470 nautical miles.

The more time Jim spends at sea, the more he distances himself from his wife. In the summer of 2017 he makes a decision in preference to the sea, which does him so much good. During this time he decides to retreat further from his business to explore the world, perhaps to circumnavigate it. But he needs a bigger yacht for that. In search of a suitable boat, he comes across the Sun Odyssey 44 DS, a deck salon yacht, big and bright, equipped like a modern apartment. The dealer convinces him to order a new yacht and takes his old Nordship in part payment. Six months later, in April 2018, Jim's new yacht is ready to be picked up in France. During that time, Jim has altered his business structure so that he only needs to communicate with his manager once a week. The rest of the week he can devote himself to sailing.

In April 2018, Jim flies to France. He hires various skippers to assist him transporting 'Acheron' in several stages from Marseilles via Sardinia and Sicily, through the Gulf of Corinth to the Aegean and finally to Kaş in the south of Turkey. In the meantime, Jim has also found a way to fulfill the promise that he gave to God when he was seventeen. For many years he had been creating beautiful art nude images working with models from around the world. Now they come on board and sail with him, and by this means find breathtaking locations in which to portray the beauty of mother nature. Land, sea, sky, and woman.

Who wants to follow Jim will find him on Instagram: @jimfurness1000. Or check his blog: www.yachtacheron.com

Never

MIKE
ELAINE

Say

Never

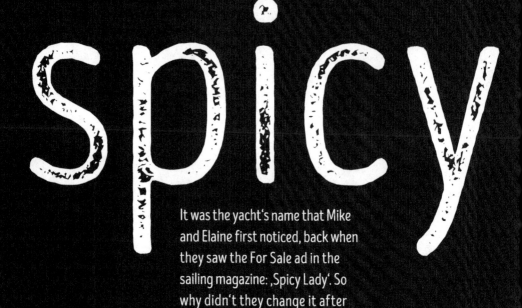

spicy

It was the yacht's name that Mike and Elaine first noticed, back when they saw the For Sale ad in the sailing magazine: ‚Spicy Lady'. So why didn't they change it after they bought the boat? „That brings bad luck," says Elaine. Plus she still likes the idea that people think Mike named the yacht after her, the ‚Spicy' lady.

BUILT: 1991
BOUGHT: 2011
PRICE: 60.000 GBP

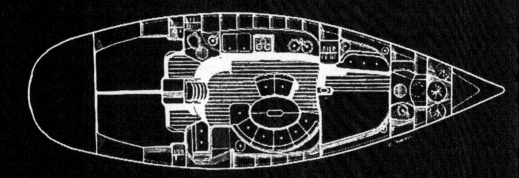

BENETEAU FIRST 45F5
length: 14,20m, beam: 4,25m, draft: 2,00m

lady

MIKE
53, ENGLAND

ELAINE
55, ENGLAND

DREAM: Sailing the world

REALITY: Saving money for 20 years

EARNINGS: Yacht deliveries

For Mike ‚Spicy Lady' was everything he'd been looking for and working towards for the last 20 years. Now he was ready to pack in work and circumnavigate the globe. That plan got put on hold for a while. For seven years Mike and Elaine have been living on their ‚Spicy Lady' in Turkey. To top up their cruising kitty, they transfer yachts across the Mediterranean. But one day their planned circumnavigation really will happen, they are sure.

The day that Mike realises the master plan for his life, he's sitting in a drab classroom somewhere on the west coast of England, not far from Liverpool. It's a theory lesson, how he hates theory lessons. But in order to gain his dive master certification he has to go through the complete process: physics, physiology and equipment are all on the syllabus. Mike has found a seat right next to the window, so he can let his eyes wander over the small harbour and the water. From up here, on the second floor, he has a good view.

He has recently returned from Tenerife, from the warm Atlantic sunshine back to wet cold Chester in north west England. He flew to the Canaries for a short vacation. And stayed. Only a month, then six. In the end it was three and a half years. He needed that time out.

Mike was in his mid-twenties at the time and he'd already put in a few hard years as a craftsman. Always in construction, always on the move, from job to job. In Tenerife he worked various jobs. At night he encouraged tourists to come in and have a drink in the pubs and clubs. During the day he distributed flyers on the beach to sun burnt and hung over holiday makers.

At the beginning of the ‚90s Las Americas in south Tenerife is for British tourists a throbbing, neon lit party zone. Just the place for a young man looking for diversion and adventure. It's a wild, excessive phase in Mike's life. He gets to know one of the DJ's called Barry Noble, who's originally from the Wirral peninsula which is not far from Mike's home town. They connect and when they're not working they spend a lot of time together hanging out around the pool, drinking beer, chatting to girls and listening to Dire Straits.

At that time neither of them suspects that 30 years later they will spend a winter together in Turkey. Each living fulltime on their own sailboat.

After three and a half years, the party life on Tenerife comes to an end for Mike. He moves back to Chester, where he grew up with his two sisters. The most famous son of the city is likely to be Daniel Craig, the blonde James Bond. Mike is back to make serious money again. Experienced craftsmen like him are always sought after, so it doesn't take long for Mike to get back into the old routine, working his way from job to job across the UK.

Mike likes Chester, his birthplace on the border with north Wales, which is known by tourists for its two-story covered arcades and Tudor-style half-timbered houses. At the gates of the city are 2000 year old Roman ruins and an amphitheater from the time when Chester was considered the most important city in England. It was the main outpost of the Romans in the fight against the Celts, who had retreated to present day Wales and fiercely resisted the roman invaders from there.

But Mike doesn't want to grow old in Chester. At least not without first experiencing something more of the world. Even though his job means he travels a lot, a different kind of wanderlust still gnaws at him. He makes good money, but the work is physically tough. You can tell the man that works hard. Mike's a wiry guy with sinewy arms. He's the type of man who never stands alone at the bar in pubs. His voice is rough from the many cigarettes he smokes, beer is his favorite drink, and not just in the evening. A sociable guy with a joke that others like to listen to. Mike is a can do guy with adventurer's genes. For Mike, Chester is not enough, he wants the whole world.

As he sits in the classroom that day, studying to be a dive master, totally bored, he looks out the window. „And then it suddenly clicked." says Mike as he snaps his fingers in front of his face. When Mike talks about that moment, his eyes light up, then a smile flits across his suntanned face. „I saw this sailing ship coming into the harbour. A man and a woman on it. I have no idea what kind of yacht that was, maybe 35, maybe 38 feet," recalls the 53-year-old. Mike continues explaining his revelation. „That was it! A floating VW bus, then I knew I wanted to live on a sailboat and sail around the world."

For a long time Mike had once again been feeling the need to break out of his daily routine. As varied as his jobs were, Monday to Friday was always the same. He was not satisfied at work. In order to earn better money, he often pulled double shifts. Always getting up early, working 12 hours a day, then in the evening, in the hotel or the apartment he drank beer. Every day was an exact copy of the day before.

At the time Mike didn't know why he was pushing himself so hard. He had neither wife nor children. No responsibility. Except for himself. Why was he grinding so hard? Was it only to have a few more pounds in his pocket to drink in the pub? Life on a sailing ship was definitely a better alternative.

From that moment on Mike has a plan: to earn as much money as possible and to get away as fast as possible. Ideally, he needs to build something using his many skills, something that will give him a steady income when he is at sea. It doesn't need to be a lot of money, Mike is satisfied with just enough. So Mike invests every penny he has buying some land in Chester to build houses on.

In the meantime, he takes on lucrative jobs all over the world. For nine months he works in Moscow, he goes to Holland and to Cyprus. He lives in Düsseldorf for three and a half years, helping to build the Movie Park in Bottrop. In Warner Bros Amusement Park in Australia, he builds a roller coaster, builds the steel structure of a 3000 seat auditorium. Always at the front of his mind is the sailboat.

Mike is already a very competent dinghy sailor, he's been sailing them since he was 10 years old. For many years he's remained loyal to the Hobie cat, sailing in a class similar to the 470s. In all kinds of wind and weather Mike heads to the coast and goes out on the water. The cold Irish Sea is his master. She punishes every little mistake with an icy shower. But if his plan to sail around the world is to be successful he knows he needs more training. He works his way through RYA sailing courses until he eventually achieves ‚offshore yacht master‘ certification.

To gain more experience, Mike works for 6 months as a sailing instructor in Southampton on the south coast of England. The craftsman from Chester becomes Mike the skipper. And then when better paying construction work comes along he is again Mike the craftsman. But the money he's saving is still not enough to escape.

One evening in his local pub he meets Elaine. This woman from Manchester with the striking eyes is the complete opposite of Mike. He is unshaven and usually wears simple T-shirts, she puts emphasis on stylish clothes, paints her fingernails in bright colors, always perfect make-up.

They chat and Elaine explains how bored she is with her office job. Mike lays out his big plans for circumnavigating the world. Elaine, a year older than Mike, can't think of anything better than running away with this man, making his dream hers too. Like a magnet, the opposites attract. Mike is excited. „If she had said she couldn't imagine a life on a sailboat, then it would've been over," he says rigorously. And laughs. As a test they charter a boat in Mallorca. Elaine not only passes Mike's baptism of fire, she enjoys her time on the water and shows plenty of competence.

Back in England, the pair browse the classifieds of yachts for sale in the sailing magazines. At this time Mike is in his 40s. He's built four houses. If he sells one, he can afford a sailboat, the monthly rental income from the other houses would provide a simple life anywhere in the world.

Mike notices an advertisement for a yacht with the catchy name ‚Spicy Lady‘. A Beneteau First 45F5, built in 1991, berthed at Bodrum in Turkey. But the price deters him: £100,000 British pounds. Too much for him and Elaine.

A month later, the next issue of Yachting Monthly is on the newsstand. Mike sees that ‚Spicy Lady‘ is still for sale, but now the price has dropped to £90,000. Still too much. More months pass until Mike's dream yacht is listed at £75,000. He calls the yacht broker, tells him he's ready to buy the boat for £60,000. If the seller agrees on the price, he'll fly out immediately to look at it. The seller agrees. A few days later, Mike and Elaine are boat owners. She is paying for his dream. This is in 2011. They keep the name 'Spicy Lady'. "Changing a boats name brings bad luck," says Elaine. She also likes that people think the name alludes to her. She laughs.

It takes two years until Mike can manage to sell one of his houses, as planned. From his other properties they can live well on board a yacht in Turkey. Turkey is inexpensive, although the marina in Bodrum is one of the most expensive in the region.

At a boat show Mike meets and chats with the manager of the newly built marina in Kaş, Turkey. He learns that for the money they're spending in Bodrum on mooring fees for a year, they can stay in Kaş for three years. In the spring of 2014 they sail the west coast of Turkey and on April 1st ‚Spicy Lady' arrives in Kaş marina. Mike secures a premium spot. Pontoon C, right on the shore directly in front of Oxygen Pub. The walk from the cockpit to the bar is not even 60 meters. Perfect for a guy who likes to drink beer and look at yachts.

Kaş has been the home of ‚Spicy Lady' for five years now. The planned circumnavigation, has been put on hold for a while. Elaine rolls her eyes: „Sometimes I have the impression we'll never get away from here." Mike is more laid back. For 20 years he had been working and waiting to buy a boat, now if it takes one or two years before the circumnavigation begins, it's not that big of a deal. Never say Never.

Mike is constantly working towards the day of departure, gradually equipping the yacht for a trip around the globe. First he had made a fully enclosed cockpit covering, which makes the cockpit an exclusive living area even in winter. From the outside it looks as if a large green cube landed on the cockpit. But Mike designed the enclosure to be robust as was proved in February 2019, when a hurricane with more than force twelve winds swept over the marina and tore several yachts sails and biminis to shreds. The cockpit enclosure of ‚Spicy Lady' was untouched by the measured 76 knots of wind speed.

Below deck, Mike has given his lady a plush carpet reminiscent of English pubs and on the wall hangs a giant TV. He has optimized the solar system to the new power requirements, installed a diesel heater, a watermaker, replaced winches, fitted electric toilets, revamped the galley area and changed all lamps to LEDs. Everyone in the marina envies his technical skills. This makes Mike a sought after person for every little problem. „Mike, can you ...?" And Mike can.

When funds are running low, Mike travels back to England for a few weeks, picks up well paid construction work again, pulling double shifts for 7 days a week. „In England," says Elaine, „we couldn't survive on our income we would have to go back to work." In Turkey, they live very well.

For some time, Mike and Elaine have been earning extra money making yacht deliveries around the Mediterranean. They have already delivered yachts several times from France or Spain to Turkey. The Corinth Canal now feels like their weekly commute.

One year ago they had a very special delivery. An Australian couple who had just bought their boat and had hardly any sailing experience asked if Mike and Elaine could help them sail their yacht from Spain to Turkey. For Mike, this delivery was an honour. Because the Australian guy was his old buddy from Tenerife - the DJ Barry Noble.

Mike and Elaine aren't big fans of social media. If you want to contact them, send them a mail: mjones007@hotmail.com

JENS

BYE BYE BURNOUT

dilly

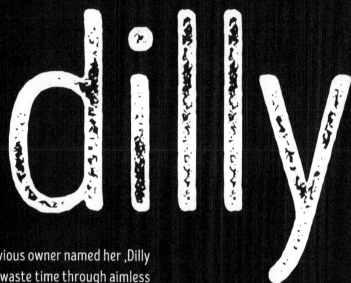

The boat's previous owner named her 'Dilly Dally': It means to waste time through aimless wandering or indecision. Because that's exactly what Jens has in mind he does not change the name. What he doesn't know is that in Turkish there is a similar sounding word 'deli'. And that means crazy! Which ironically also fits.

BUILT: 1988
BOUGHT: 2018
PRICE: 55.000 GBP

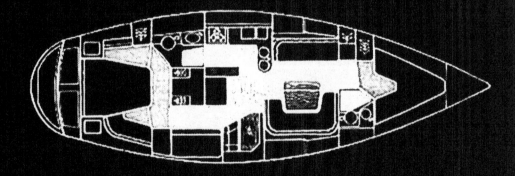

MOODY 425
length: 12,70m, beam: 4,07m, draft: 1,40m

dally

JENS

47, GERMANY

PROFESSION: Author

PASSION: Coffee and Cigarettes

PLAN: To have no plan

PARANOIA: Panic attacks

A complete burnout with anxiety and panic attacks makes the journalist realize that he has to change everything. At this time his own mind causes him to be a virtual prisoner in his own apartment, unable to step outside the front door. Only the longing for a new, different life gives him the strength to make a radical change. In mid 2018 he quits his job, sells his apartment and buys a sail boat in Turkey. The sea is now his therapist.

It's like a little Christmas miracle. We meet on Christmas Eve morning as new friends, Dagmar and Oliver, come on board 'Dilly-Dally' for a day trip, despite Dagmar's fear of seasickness. They are a German couple who are on their way to Mongolia with their off-road vehicle and stop in Kaş for a few weeks. Aannsha and Barry, the two „gray nomads" from Australia, who are berthed in the town harbor on board 'A B Sea', stroll along the pontoon to also climb on board. Of course Mark, the lovably quirky South African, our Mr. Sunshine, who is two berths up from me on his boat 'Zinga' completes the group. He brings Ruth along, a German friend who lives half the year in Turkey, the other half in Frankfurt.

With seven people on board, we leave the harbor in bright sunshine and smooth waters. Mark informs Kaş Marina that we're leaving, properly by radio. Well, almost: „Kaş-Marina, Kaş-Marina, Kaş-Marina, this is Dilly-Dally, Dilly-Dally, Dilly-Dally. We are leaving for a wonderful sail on this lovely day. We have lots of beer and wine on board, if you want, join us. Merry Christmas." Kaş Marina replies with a friendly: „Have fun!" As we glide past the tip of the pontoon the marineros wink at us jealously.

We motor along the peninsula, admiring the pretty villas that cling to the hills like colorful Lego bricks and eat breakfast consisting of delicious tahini filled sesame scrolls from Simit bakery. After one and a half hours we've reached our destination: Limanağzı. A beautiful bay near the town harbor, popular with divers because at the bottom of the sea lies an old World War II DC-3 plane wreck.

We drop anchor at a depth of 18 meters, watching it through the crystal clear water as it approaches the bottom and digs into the sand. When the engine stops there is an almost contemplative silence. Small ripples softly splash against the side of the ship, a single seagull screeches, a bird of prey circles over the steep cliff, into which the ancient Lycians carved their rock tombs. And we pop open beer bottles. The women lounge in the sun on the quarterdeck, the men fly drones. The galley is constantly serving new delicacies that each of us has brought with us. My first Christmas on board. And in shorts! Glorious.

It doesn't take long for a slender mast to appear on the horizon, quickly growing larger. Ken, a Brit who's raised the smallest possible national flag in protest against Brexit, is approaching. He comes alongside 'Dilly-Dally' at an athletic pace, wildly rafting 'Asteria', which we've now jokingly renamed 'Hysteria'. He opens a can of Efes beer, takes a long sip, spreads his arms and calls: „Merry Christmas!" Mark, who has found the volume control of the speakers, climbs onto the foredeck to pounding bass, answers, what else: „What a beautiful day!"

After another hour, there are three yachts rafted together. Ismail on his yacht 'Wanda' has arrived with the boys from Oxygen Pub, some girls and their pet dog, to have a BBQ on Christmas Eve. We celebrate Christmas with 15 people. Swimming, paddling, chatting, just having a good time away from the hustle and bustle found on highways and in living rooms throughout Germany during this period.

We raise the anchor only as the evening sun disappears slowly behind the hills of the Greek island of Kastellorizo and sail in the refreshing breeze towards the glowing red ball. When we arrive in the dark at the marina, we spontaneously decide to end the evening on board. We collect supplies from our boats and conjure up a simple banquet.

This Christmas Eve is like a little Christmas miracle, and not just for me. Barry is also amazed the following morning that he managed to stagger back onto his yacht across 'A B Sea's' wobbly gangway. But the miracle I'm referring to is something else entirely: Exactly a year ago, I was sitting alone in my Berlin apartment on Christmas Eve. Unable to leave the house. Anxiety and panic attacks making me a prisoner of myself.

In the afternoon I tried to take the train to my parents. It didn't work. I couldn't leave the house. I turned back in the stairwell. Tachycardia, dizziness, nausea. My legs failed. There were mental obstacles everywhere. And now, a year later here I am, in Turkey, living on a boat and enjoying the relaxed festivities. In the evening, after the last guests have left 'Dilly-Dally', with much giggling, laughing and some staggering, I realize how much my life has changed over the past twelve months. I had gone through hell. And landed in heaven on earth. It could have been so different.

On the day of my collapse, it smells like cheesecake in my car. I am on my way to the editorial office of the business magazine Capital at the Tiergarten in Berlin. After the Financial Times Germany was discontinued because it was chronically deep in debt, I switched jobs as a reporter from Hamburg to Berlin. I mainly researched economic crimes. My texts were nominated for several journalist awards and I won a few. I loved my job. But that day I wouldn't arrive at the editorial office. Nor the next day, nor even in the coming weeks and months.

At an intersection, the traffic light jumped to red. My heart was racing, beads of sweat were forming on my forehead. I felt like I was falling over. I sat there. My field of vision had narrowed. The background noise of the morning madness on the streets was deafening and silent at the same time. And then there was this barrier in my head, like an infinitely high wall, right in front of me. I flicked the indicator, left the route that led to work, and only calmed down when I stopped at my family doctor's door. It was a Monday mid-November 2017.

I'd had a panic attack. Not the first one in my life. But this time, I sensed it was different. Worse. Permanent. For the past two years I'd been getting worse and worse each month. Nobody noticed though. Because I hid it. From others. But above all, I hid it from myself. I didn't tolerate weakness. This wasn't allowed, so it wasn't happening. In my world burnout was something only weaklings suffered. It was for quitters. I defined myself through my accomplishments. As a teenager, I was a lightweight rower, training every day like a madman, and was twice German champion in the quads and eights. That meant besides hard daily training, a special diet was included. Fasting for success. No problem.

While studying in Würzburg I lost my edge. Celebrating, drinking, I started smoking. No sport. I quickly added a few kilos. Besides studying, I worked as a freelance journalist, earning good money for a student. And because I had never learned to say no, I took on more and

more work. On the weekends, I either wrote, or drove for hours to visit my girlfriend in Munich. We celebrated a lot, allowing ourselves little rest. We were young and hungry for life. Then I snapped. In the university. Bam. Right in front of the lecturer. Shortly after that, I had the first panic attacks. Most at the cashier in the supermarket. Or in a traffic jam. Whenever I could not control the pace. I didn't really take the attacks seriously. Therapy? I'm not crazy!

I started sports again, at least moderately. Then bought an old motorhome and drove to Palestine. Through Turkey, through Syria and then Jordan. I studied Arabic and Islamic Studies with a focus on Middle East Conflict. There with the refugee camps in the West Bank and even more so in the Gaza Strip, my panic attack problems seemed so tiny. In a bizarre way, the surrounding misery helped me to forget my own problems. Over 20 years later, my therapist would say that this behavior is typical for me. Repressing instead of processing. But it worked, back then.

When the symptoms returned two years ago, I ignored them again. I will function, somehow. But I sensed that something was wrong, constantly felt exhausted and became distracted more and more often. In my job as well as during my free time. Every other weekend I drove 1000 kilometers along the highway to landsailing regattas at Sankt Peter-Ording or elsewhere in Europe, was a member of the Board for Landsailors for eight years, developed their PR and helped organize European and World Championships. In Berlin, I extended myself to become part of the Advisory Board of the WEG for my apartment building. The other owners in the complex had quickly disappeared when it came to a vote. And when the loft conversion became a disaster, everyone had a complaint. But instead of contacting the owner, it was much easier for them to use the advisory board as a punching bag. Jens would fix that. I just had to do it. And I knew that if I did something myself, then it would be fine. At least that's what I thought. Pride comes just before a fall.

My private life had been a rollercoaster ride for years. And Berlin? I didn't like it that much. Too big, too hectic, too aggressive. A city full of wannabes and complainers, but few doers. Also, journalism changed a lot. Less readers, less advertisements, smaller teams while workloads got larger. „Can you ...?" „Sure!" I accepted every task.

All this cost energy. Unbelievable amounts of energy. The flame that fueled me was getting smaller and smaller. And that day in November 2017, I knew it had gone out. The doctor was surprised. Most people with my symptoms believe it's a chronic physical condition. They crave a disease that's explainable. I just stated, „It's my head."

My dearest wish: a hospital stay. I was afraid I couldn't do it alone. But those who have never had therapy, don't get paid immediately for an expensive hospital stay. Even as a private patient. And so I was sent home with a yellow note in my hand. Have a rest. The diagnosis: burnout, panic attacks, anxiety, agoraphobia. Or as the neurologist later said: „Well, congratulations, because you've got the whole package."

The worst time of my life had begun. I was a prisoner of myself, imprisoned in my apartment. Getting to the mailbox was sometimes unmanageable. Some days I wasn't even able to make phone calls. Too exhausting. Too grueling. Too impossible.

And me. I had reported from Afghanistan, lived in the Middle East, interviewed terrorists and exposed economic spies. I'd put people in jail and stood trial because companies sent out their lawyers rather than admit they'd screwed up. I was threatened and intimidated. Everything began to mount up. Soaking into me like water splashing onto a dry suit. I was drowning. And suddenly I wasn't even able to go to the supermarket or corner store.

Anxiety is difficult to understand if you haven't experienced it yourself. Nothing functions any more. There were days when I had to make three or four attempts to get out of the apartment. I had to drive to the supermarket that was only 400 meters away. Walking or cycling was impossible. I continued to feel that I was falling over. When I arrived at the supermarket by car, it didn't mean that I'd made it into the supermarket. Often the sight of the door was enough to trigger a panic attack. So I'd reverse. Back to the apartment. Hoping not to collapse on the way.

Once I'd made it into the shop, the aisles seemed to me to be too long for me to penetrate even halfway. Then I clung to the trolley, like seniors to a walking frame. And when I arrived at the cash register, I often had only half of the items on my shopping list. I didn't have the strength for any more.

The next blow came shortly before Christmas. My health insurance finally refused to fund the hoped for hospital stay. The reason: I should try outpatient therapy first. Or medication. I attempted to continue without any kind of pills.

Then came Christmas. The train tickets were booked and Berlin Ostbahnhof station was only a stone's throw away. Just five minutes by car. I didn't even reach the street in front of my house. The journey to my parents ended at the staircase. It was the same on New Year's Eve. I wanted to party with friends. But the fetters of fear were too strong, I simply couldn't overcome them.

It is thanks to only one friend, that I managed to leave the house every now and then. „I won't visit you anymore." she said. „We can meet, but only in cafes or restaurants." All places I found particularly hard to navigate. But those were her conditions. And indeed, the plan worked. Although not without a lot of overcoming and effort. And it wasn't always successful. But most times it did though. I realized that I can fight my fears. Only if I want to, if it's something that really means a lot to me.

During this time I discovered the 'SV Delos' YouTube channel. Two brothers who have been sailing around the world with their friends for nine years. I was fascinated by the films they put on the Internet. I watched them one by one. There were just under 200. I was so excited that I wrote an article about the ‚Delos'-Crew later on. Because the crew not only lives their dream, they also live from their dream. Even for a business magazine, that was interesting.

I have spent all my holidays on boats since childhood. My parents had a sailboat. First a little Neptune 22, later a Swedish Arkona 32. But because sailing with parents can be a bit tiresome for a teenager, I got the necessary sailing licenses when I was 16 years old to go sailing with friends on the Baltic Sea. My parents trusted me with their boat. And regretted it again and again.

Once I bumped the boat against the jetty when mooring in a storm (forward and reverse are so close together), once the spray hood tore, once the engine failed, once a hatch broke. And even the saloon table broke, when a wave lifted my buddy off balance and he fell on the table. After that I was banned from using the boat.

But even when I studied in Würzburg, a small town in Bavaria, it wasn't possible without sailing. I first bought a corsair, then a 505er, then a 15er yawl cruiser. When I moved to Hamburg, I sailed with the dinghy of the publishing house on the Alster. And discovered a passion for landsailing in Sankt Peter-Ording. Ten years ago, I took part in my first European Championship. And surprisingly came home with a silver medal in the team class. But that is another story. It certainly had nothing to do with outstanding performance. Later I changed classes, bought a total of three land sailing yachts, and took part in some European and World Championships. So sailing has been with me all my life. Even if it was never my focus.

And even on my last stop in Berlin, it wasn't long before I put a 20er yawl cruiser on Lake Müggelsee. I also chartered yachts in the Mediterranean for 13 years as a skipper with friends. Balearic Islands, Croatia, Greece - but mostly

CHRISTMAS 2018
LIMANAGZI WANDA DILLY-DALLY ASTERIA

in Turkey. We always found Turkey the most beautiful. And as I lay there, on my couch, trapped within myself, watching the videos of 'SV Delos', the yearning grew in me. The dream of becoming a liveaboard and casting off, to anchor wherever I pleased became a concrete plan. And the plan gave me courage - the lethargy gave way to life.

To earth myself, I decided to go to the water. I talked to my therapist about my great project, expecting approval, maybe even applause. He just looked at me, irritated. It wasn't until I mentioned that I wanted to sell my apartment that he was hooked. The conversation was no longer about my salvation, but about location, square footage, equipment and price. Shortly thereafter, I finished the sessions with him. I had found a better therapist: the yearning for the sea.

I crunched numbers for days. Can I afford to do this? And how do I earn my bread and butter? I can't do much more than write, but I can do it from anywhere in the world, so I decided that change of tack wasn't difficult. It was clear to me that even if I were to go broke after a few years, I would undoubtedly have experienced some wonderful years on the water, which nobody could take away from me. But if I tried to keep going like before, tormenting myself towards retirement, I probably wouldn't see any wonderful years.

With the sale of my apartment, which had already doubled in price since moving in four years perviously, there was enough cash in the bank to buy a suitable boat and to keep me afloat for quite some time. The more concrete my plans became, the better I felt. When I returned to work at the beginning of March, I had long since mentally quit my job. A short time later I made it official. It was like a liberation.

My whole life fit into a VW Golf. When I closed the door to my apartment in late August 2018, I left more than half of my life behind. All the furniture, shelves, even the pictures on the walls and the cutlery in the kitchen drawer. I took only a few clothes, laptop, camera and a few books. I put most of it under my parents' roof. All I took from my old life to my new life were two full cases. I didn't need anything more.

I had thought that I'd be gripped by sadness if I left the apartment as if I were going on a weekend trip. But I felt nothing! Except relief. I had expected the day would come when I'd doubt whether the decision to quit a permanent job was the right one. It never arrived.

A short time later, when I traveled to Turkey with my buddy Stephan Boden to buy a boat and found 'Dilly-Dally', I was so happy. It was the third boat on a list of ten favorites compiled from an Internet search. But when I saw this Moody 425 for the first time, rocking gently in the waves at anchor in the bay of Marmaris, I knew immediately that my search was over. After a sea trial the next day, I sealed the deal.

Despite all the political turmoil, it was clear to me from the beginning that my restart would be in Turkey. In Kaş, the place I visited for the first time in 1992 and which captivated me then. I like the country, the people, the landscape. During my studies, I spent a summer semester in Izmir, completing a language scholarship, most of which unfortunately hasn't stuck - only my restaurant Turkish is still reasonably usable. So at least I won't starve. When I landed at Bodrum Airport very early one morning at the beginning of October, I might have had half an hour of sleep. But there was no signs of tiredness. The journey by rental car to Marmaris took one and a half hours. I enjoyed every winding kilometer across the mountains.

I bought 'Dilly-Dally' through Sunbird agency. The office was my first port of call that morning and all the documents were there. The purchase had gone smoothly. Peter, the yacht broker, a tall man, born in Zambia, endowed with a fine British humor and the serenity of a Southerner, proved to be an absolute stroke of luck.

While traveling to the landsailing world championships in Sankt Peter-Ording at the end of September, he'd transferred the boat to the Marmaris Yacht Marina at the other end of the bay, taken care of provisional insurance, cheap mooring and arranged a boat technician for me. 'Dilly-Dally' needed custom-made davits with a solar system mounted on top. That's how I met Brian, a Brit who, like Peter, has been living in Marmaris for years.

On my first night aboard 'Dilly-Dally' I slept for twelve hours. As long as I had slept in years. And the first thing I thought about the next morning was a nice hot cup of instant coffee. One and a half spoons, hot water from the whistling kettle and a dash of milk. For me, the simplest of all coffees tastes like sailing. Just as Delial smells like a summer vacation.

I have been living on the boat for eight months now.
I haven't regretted it one day. Some days have been uncomfortable. Like when it stormed. When heavy thunderstorms raged over the marina. When it was bitterly
cold at night and the next morning the condensation
dripped from the hatches. But then, after the first coffee
and the view from the hatch to this stunning natural
scenery, the world was beautiful again. Especially when
my neighbor Mark called, „Good morning, SIR! What a
wonderful day!" And then laughed out loud.

I've chosen Kaş as home port until next spring, when
I'll sail along the Turkish south coast, with new and old
friends sharing my life. My plan is not to have a plan.
But to take it easy. I feel completely fit again. Physically
as well as mentally. The sea has saved me. Even if there
are situations in which something like panic rises in me.
But those moments are becoming rarer. And they don't
affect me anymore. I'm almost happy about them because
they remind me how bad I was a year ago.

The plop of flip-flops on my feet is the soundtrack to my
new life. It is a steady pace, calm, without hurry and
rush, adapted to the environment, to the people, to the
splashing of the waves on the shore. It sounds good. And
it feels so much better.

The easiest way to follow Jens is to have a look at his website:
www.brambusch-macht-blau.de.

SPRING 2018

INSPIRATION
SV DELOS

delos

BUILT: 2000
BOUGHT: 2008
PRICE: 400.000 $

Brian liked the name of the yacht and decided to keep it. Delos is a Greek island steeped in Greek mythology. When Zeus betrayed his wife with a human woman and she gave birth to twins, the horned one banished the babies from every country in the world. Zeus' buddy Poseidon had an idea. He separated part of his underwater kingdom and created a new island where the illegitimate children could live. The island was named Delos.

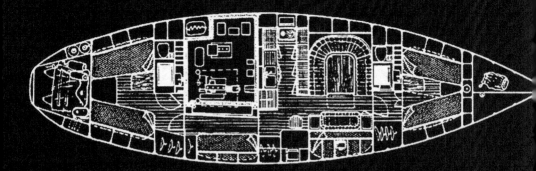

AMEL SUPERMARAMU
length: 16m, beam: 4,60m, draft: 2,05m

BRIAN

<--------- BROTHERS --------->

BRADY

Brian started in August 2009 in Seattle

few months later Brady boarded in Mexico - and never left

MARRIED

GIRL FRIEND

2011 in New Zealand Karin joined the Crew

2017 Alex joined Delos in South Africa

KARIN

ALEX

STARTED: Ten years ago

FINANCED: By videos

REACH: Up to 5 million people

No, ‚Delos' is not sailing around the Mediterranean or anywhere near Turkey. She is currently heading for Portugal. The explanation as to why Brian Trautman and the crew of ‚Delos' are included as a bonus chapter is simply because their story was the inspirational spark for several of the other contributors' stories in this book.

First there is this fragrance. The South Atlantic suddenly smells different, somehow like wood and soil. Fifteen days ago and 2,240 miles back SV Delos left the island of Ascension, halfway between South America and Africa. Since then there has been nothing but water. At dawn under full sail, the yacht plows through the waves. At first it seems as if there are gray clouds sticking to the horizon, just waiting to be dissolved by the sun. But with each passing minute, they continue to rise out of the sea, taking on contours and colours and turning to stone. Brazil!

„That was an incredibly moving moment," says Brian, a man with a full beard and windruffled hair, who could easily get an extras role in every pirate movie. Nearly ten years ago, the former Microsoft manager in Seattle had sailed away, always to the southwest, around the earth, without a plan and bankruptcy always not too far behind. Now the 44-year-old smells America again.

Thousands of sailors, dreamers and sofa adventurers eagerly await Fridays. That's the day that Brian and his friends post a new episode of their trip around the world on YouTube. There are already more than 200 episodes. Brian, his brother Brady and their partners Karin and Alex are now something like maritime soap opera stars, with ratings as high or higher than some TV shows.

There are hardly any bad times on Delos. No drama, no quarrel, no script. Just the authentic life of young people who live their dream. Some of the half-hour episodes have been viewed more than five million times. Svdelos.com is thus the most successful sailing video blog in the world, and the fascination of the videos lies in their presentation style.

It has always been a dream of people to explore the world, to discover foreign cultures, to survive adventures. But only very few have the courage to leave. Most are more than happy to live vicariously through the dreams of others. In a fast paced world in which you can fly half-way around the world in twelve hours, globetrotters who move around the globe at seven knots of slow motion appear as the envied alternative to the hustle and bustle of our times.

Brian was not born a sailor. The only knot he knew was the tie knot. He was a business world type in a dark suit, clean shaven and perfect hair. His life ticked along at fifty to ten. Fifty minutes meetings, ten minutes preparation for the next. Then rinse and repeat.

The day Brian decided to change his life, he stared at an organization chart. It hung in his boss's office at the Microsoft Technology Center in Seattle. At the top was Bill Gates, next to Steve Ballmer. Then dozens of other names. It was the management structure of the group. His boss pointed to a position high up: „My name should stand there." That was his dream. „I thought that was sad," says Brian today. „How can a lifelong dream be to have your name on an organization chart?"

Brian started reading books about circumnavigators, even though he could not actually sail. As Microsoft shed workers, he founded an IT consultancy with some friends and became responsible for 35 employees. During this time he worked almost around the clock. „We made a lot of money," says Brian. Then came the financial crisis. In three months they lost 90 percent of their turnover. „If not now, when?" Brian thinks. He has by now learned to sail on small dinghies on the lakes in the north of the USA, now he is looking for a suitable boat for his trip around the world. And finds SV Delos in Seattle.

A Supermaramu of the French shipyard Amel, 16 metres long, with all the comforts. Amel is famous for building blue water sailboats. But even pre-owned the yacht costs $400,000. Brian sells his house, his cars. It is not enough. So he takes out a ship's mortgage, so that he still has enough money in the cruising kitty for about two years.

In September 2009 he sets sail with his then girlfriend. From Seattle and goes to Mexico. There his younger brother Brady comes on board, a student and a trained diving instructor. Actually, he only wants to help Brian with the passage to Tahiti. But he will end up staying onboard for many years to come.

In October 2010 Delos reaches New Zealand. „The first few months were strange," says Brian. „Suddenly life's pace went from100 to zero, I had a problem coping with that. I felt guilty about doing nothing." His girlfriend does not enjoy the new life on board. She leaves the yacht. The Trautman brothers do not stay alone for long though. The Swede Karin comes on board for a weekend - and stays. As you read this, Brian and Karin are married. Brady meets a New Zealander and she travels the world with them for four years.

From Auckland the new group of friends are heading to Australia. „I was broke for the first time," says Brian. Even though each of them can afford only $500 a month, the

mortgage on the ship, the insurance and the maintenance costs are eating away at their savings.

In Australia, Brian works again for his former company.
As a kind of digital nomad. From the boat. But it's no fun.
The rest of the crew works in restaurants or as a crew on
mega yachts. After a year, they have enough cash in the
kitty to continue sailing. But they only make it as far as
the Philippines, then they are broke again. The dream of
escaping seems to have burst.

When Brian checks his finances, he discovers, in addition
to many big red numbers, a small black one. YouTube has
transferred a handful of dollars. For what? They had up-
loaded some videos for friends, badly filmed and edited
very amateurishly. Nevertheless, the videos were clicked
hundreds of times. Strangers encourage the crew of
Delos to continue.

„That was the start of our lifestyle business," says Brian. The
idea: „If we already make a few bucks with a few hundred
clicks, why not try a few thousand clicks?" He says. „When
we had a few thousand clicks, we wanted tens of thousands."

But for this the videos need a much better quality. Watching YouTube tutorials, they learn how to edit professionally. But they need better software and cameras. So far, they
have filmed with a $200 camcorder. Then they discover
the crowd funding platform Patreon. Artists and musicians finance their projects here. Why not travelers making videos too?

So Brian writes, „We love sailing. We love traveling. And
we love to make videos of it. With your support, we want

to buy better video equipment and make better films." Paying five dollars a video gets the rank of „swab" and you get early access to each new video, plus bonus material. But there are also extra Patron tiers for „mate" or „pirates" - the higher the total subscription per video, the more extras, right up to the „on-board visit".

The idea takes off. One of the first supporters wants to pay $250 per film. Brian believes it's a mistake. He writes to the man. But it is not an oversight. The „Delos" crew do exactly what he always dreamed of, he writes back. Now he is ill and will never be able to leave his bed again. The videos made him so happy that he wants to support the project. „It's going to take your breath away," says Brian.

The professionalism of the videos encourages more paying supporters. There is almost always a camera shooting something on board. The videos thrive on breathtaking images on, under and over the water, on land excursions, on the curiosity of everything foreign. But also topics such as the pollution of the oceans or overfishing are touched upon.

However, it is mainly about life on board. Sometimes storms on the high seas have to be weathered, sometimes seasickness gnaws at the nerves. Twice Delos was attacked. But no hero stories are written, Brian and his friends do not act as daredevils or gamblers. Rather, the crew is struggling with the perils of everyday life. With clogged toilets, a defective tax system or with authorities. Above all, they enjoy their lives in the most beautiful places in the world. The concept works.

Nearly 2,000 patrons now pay around $14,400 - per video. Three episodes appear on average per month, which makes over half a million dollars a year. In addition there are revenues from YouTube. However, Brian refrained from advertising that interrupts the flow of the videos, even if that would flush more money into the sailing kitty. „We are so thankful that our supporters make our adventure possible. We can even pay for our pension. We do not need anything more."

But the holiday becomes a job. „Some days we work twelve hours," says Brian. Other days, they enjoy life without a camera. On average, each crewmember dedicates three to four hours daily to the work: filming, editing, writing blogs, serving social media channels.

Whenever they have internet coverage, they post several posts a day on Facebook and Instagram. When Brian jumps into a pool with a belly flop on a birthday video, it gets 37,000 likes. Hundreds of congratulations are sent. And many beers. Brian laughs. „We love beer." In the US, it's quite normal to buy a beer in the bar for a guy who has an exciting or interesting story to tell. So they had decided to place a button on their website. „Buy us a beer" is here. If you click on it, you can transfer a few dollars for beer. Each video ends with the crew drinking beer on a secluded beach in the sunset and the call to buy a beer. „It's unbelievable, but we've already been given thousands of beers in this way," says the skipper of „Delos".

The Delos tribe as Brian calls the supporters, always delivers new ideas. When the crew wore shirts with the logo of the yacht, there are inquiries as to whether the shirts should also be available for purchase. Now, the sailors have an online shop with T-shirts, hats, cups, towels and of course beer holders.

The lifestyle business is booming. Patrons who join the tiers with an ,invite on board' can sail for free, all they have to pay for are their flights. More than 60 guests from 14 nations have already been on board. Some for a few days, some for months.

More and more businesses are becoming aware of Delos. Their Instagram account has 117,000 followers. A fine, sharp target group. Sailors usually have a bit more money to spend than the average person. But Brian refuses to advertise on his channels for products like sunglasses or clothes behind which he does not stand or which do not suit him and his friends. „We are not classic influencers," he says.

But there are exceptions. When they have a generator failure in South Africa, a manufacturer sends a new generator. A sail maker provides Delos with new sails. „These are products we stand behind," says Brian. Bags were made from the old sails, which were signed and sold by the crew - the proceeds donated to charities. In general, the crew passes on 20 percent of their income to social and environmental projects.

Last summer was turbulent. Even with Delos in the Caribbean on dry land. After years in the water, she needed to be thoroughly overhauled. That's enough time for the crew to take a vacation. They visit their relatives in the US and Sweden, go on holiday in Iceland. And are guests on board another sailboat, which takes them on a polar expedition to the eternal ice. Brian gets engaged to Karin, the Swede who came on a weekend trip seven years ago. In the winter, it's back to the Caribbean.

The sweat runs in streams. In Grenada, the small Caribbean state with the colourful little houses, at noon the sun burns in the sky at over 30 degrees, the air is damp as a wet sponge. Not the best conditions for boat maintenance. Although the Delos crew could now afford to commission work on the boat, they do everything themselves. This is how they get to know their yacht, know exactly what to do in case of emergencies and repairs. And also make interesting and entertaining tutorials, which they publish on YouTube for free.

Brian and Brady quickly installed the new solar system, replaced the batteries with modern lithium batteries, sanded the hull and prepared it for the new antifouling. Hard work. But Brian wears a permanent smile on his face. Finally he is back home. On his Delos.

There are many plans for the future. Of course, at sea. „Back to an office job? No way. That's certainly not the plan!" Brian says and shakes his head. There may be a „Delos 2", he reveals. Maybe an historic ship that they have to restore first. Maybe a new one, it just depends on a lot of factors. Several shipyards want to cooperate with them. But there's a lot to consider. The latest planned destination is Japan. „We will take the longest possible route," says Brian. „We have time." Why Japan? „We wanted to go there last time. But we were just too broke. „

Whether it works out this time, is still in the stars. Brian and Karin are married and are expecting a baby. They will go ashore for a few months and will be dedicating some time to their newborn in Sweden.

Meanwhile, Brady and Alex are taking care of Delos. Through the social media, they have called for young sailing enthusiasts to apply for a transatlantic passage from Florida to the Azores. The only requirements: You should be between 16 and 22 years old and enjoy sailing. The cost of the trip is sponsored by the Delos project. Thousands of applications were received. 16 young people from all over the world made it to the final selection. So the journey on Delos continues. Even though Captain Brian and Karin are staying ashore for the time being.

You will find Delos on all social media channels. The easiest way to follow the adventures is to a have a look at their website: www.svdelos.com

Thanks to the Oxygen-Crew, here on „Wanda" on Christmas Eve 2018, for always supporting us with a cold beer.

Thanks to everyone involved!

For the great time.
For friendship!
For the nice evenings!

And especially for the willingness to share your story.

Fair winds!

Printed in Great Britain
by Amazon

10971375R10095